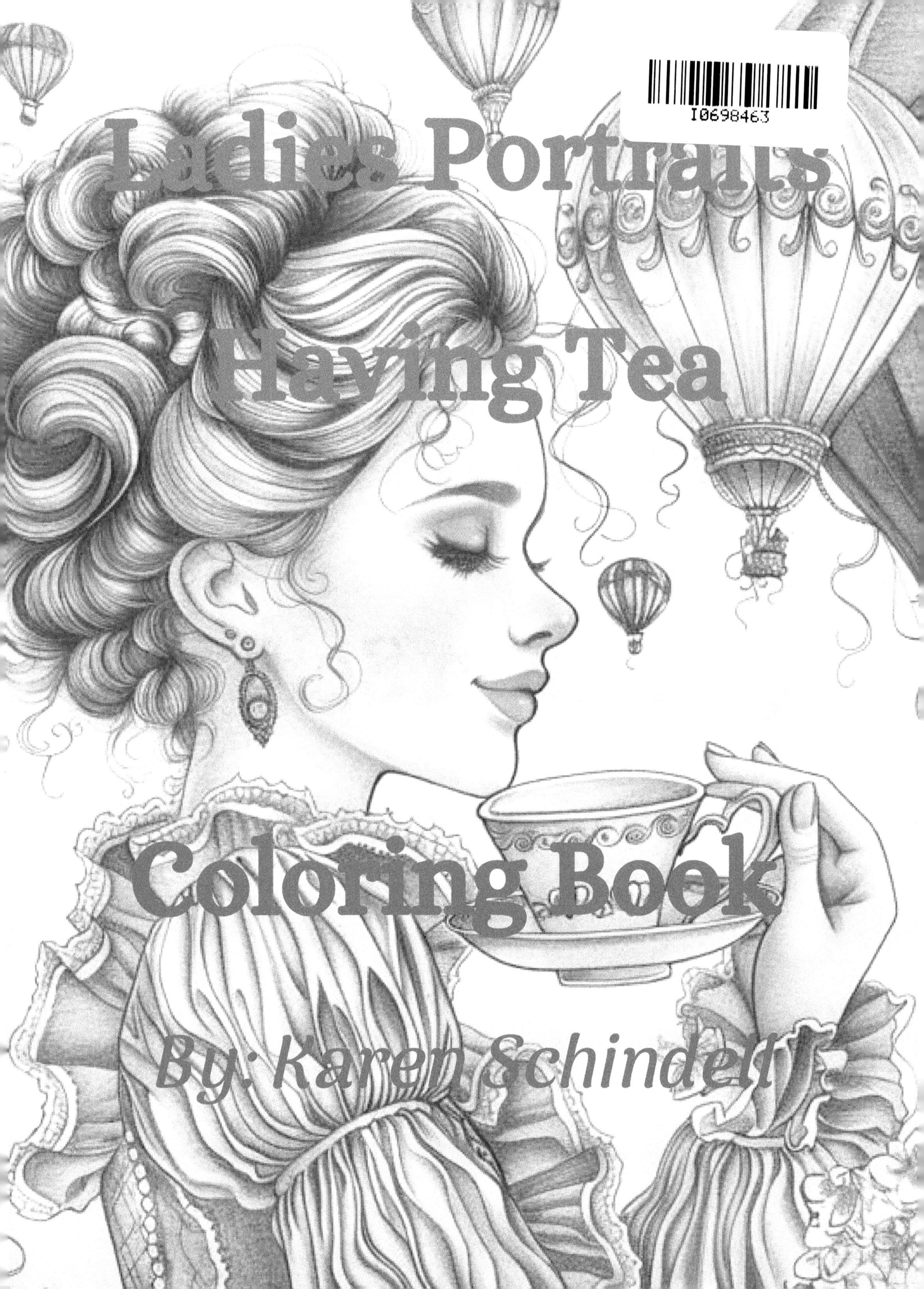

Ladies Portraits
Having Tea
Coloring Book
By: Karen Schindell

Copywritten 2024

By: Karen Schindell

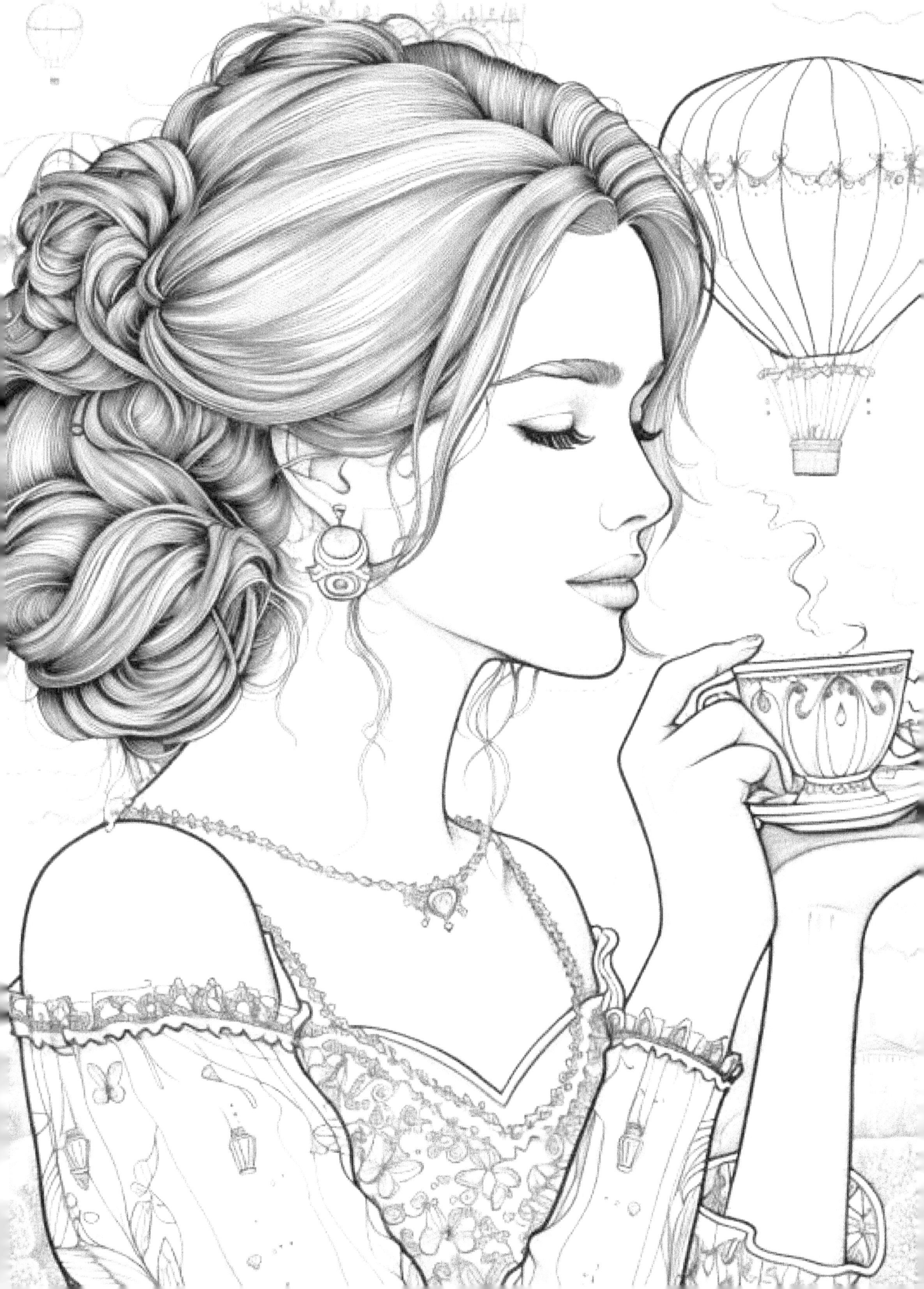

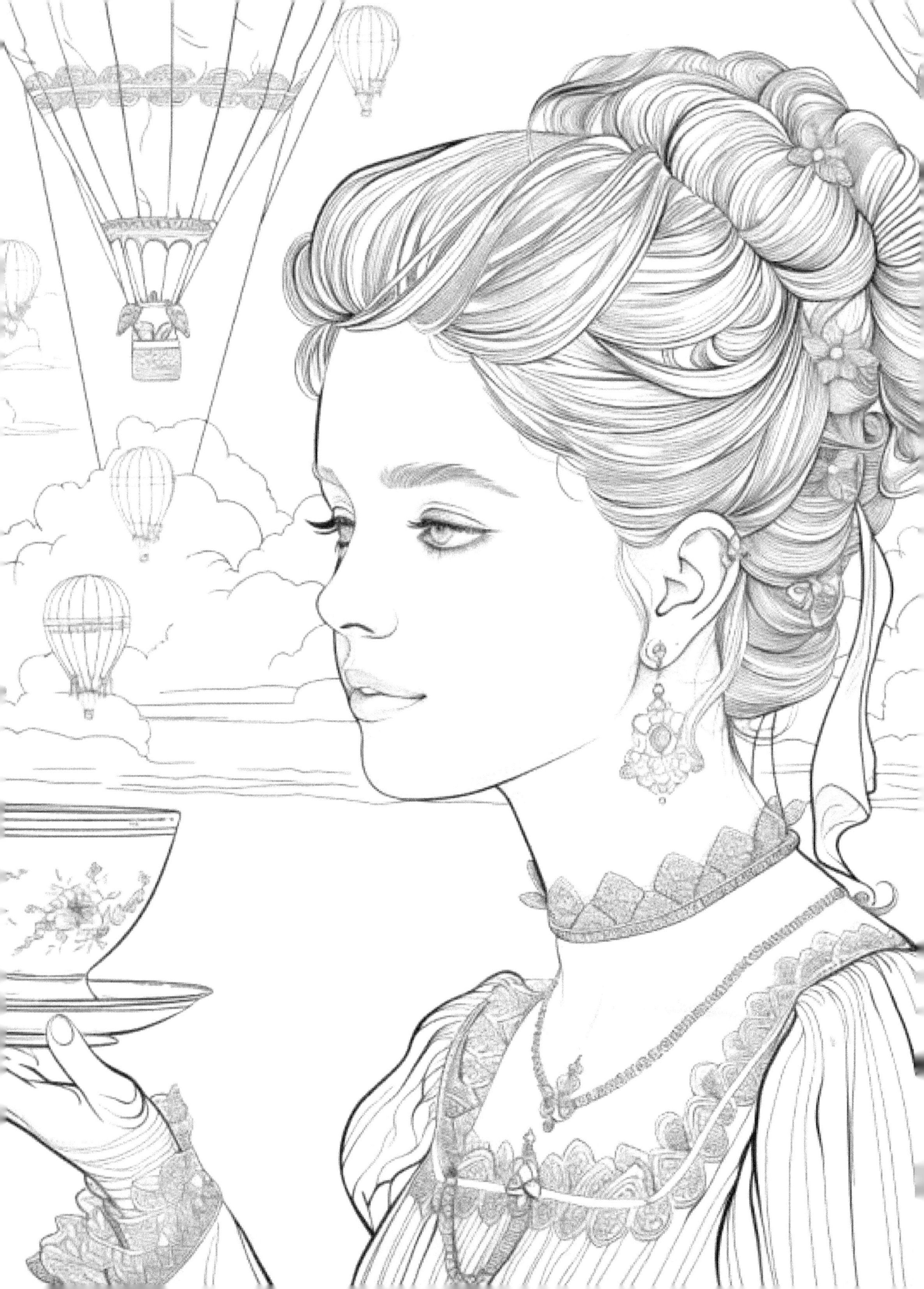

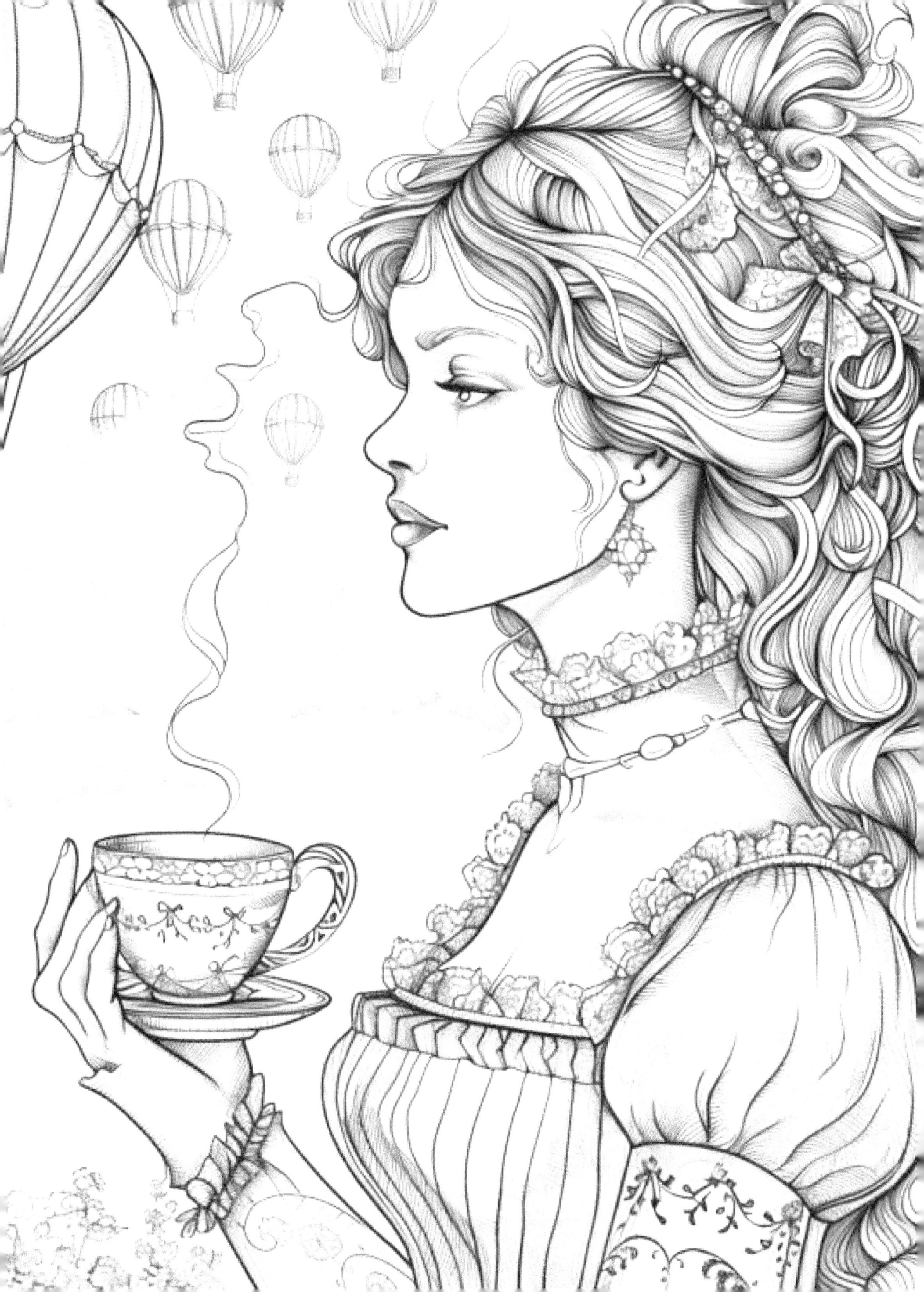

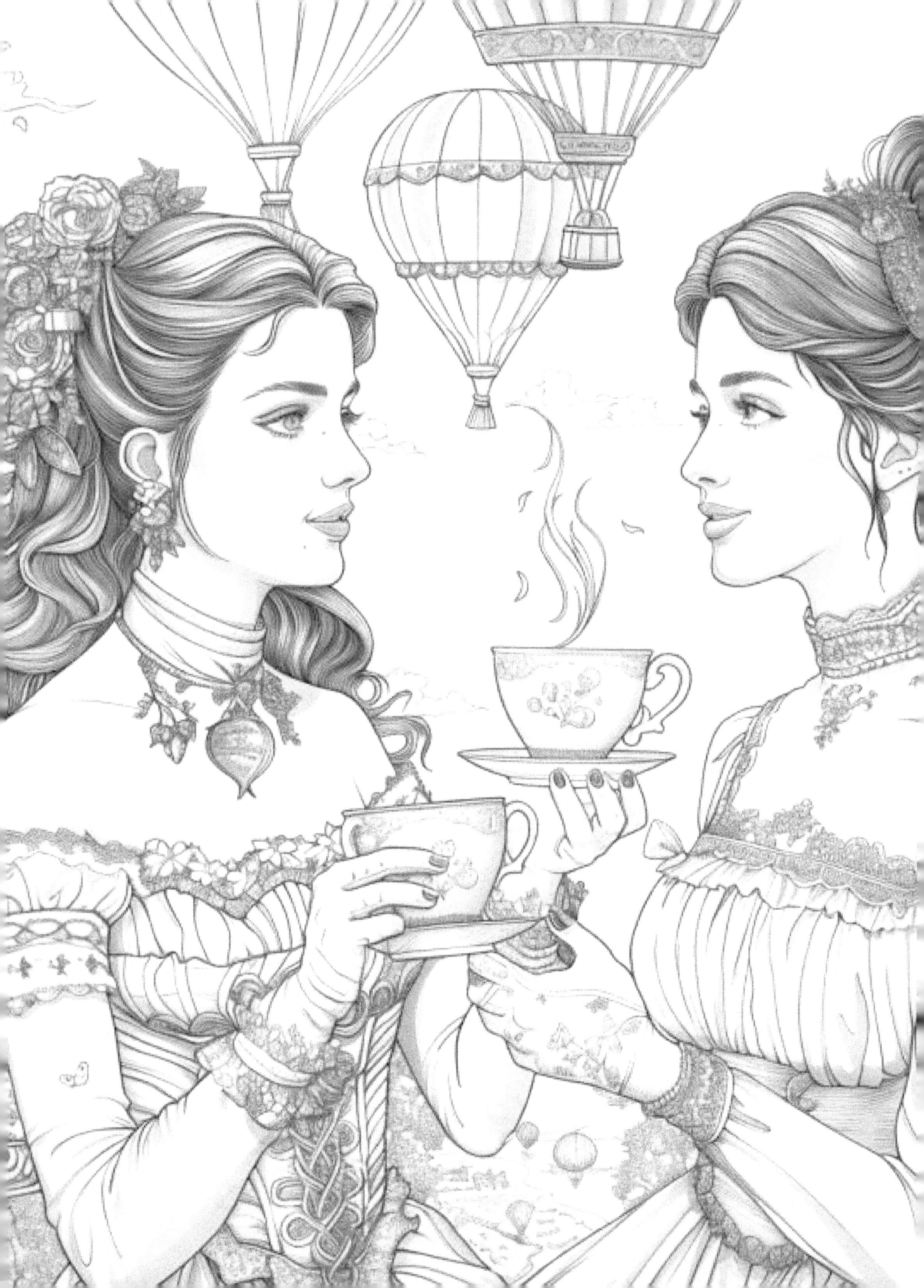

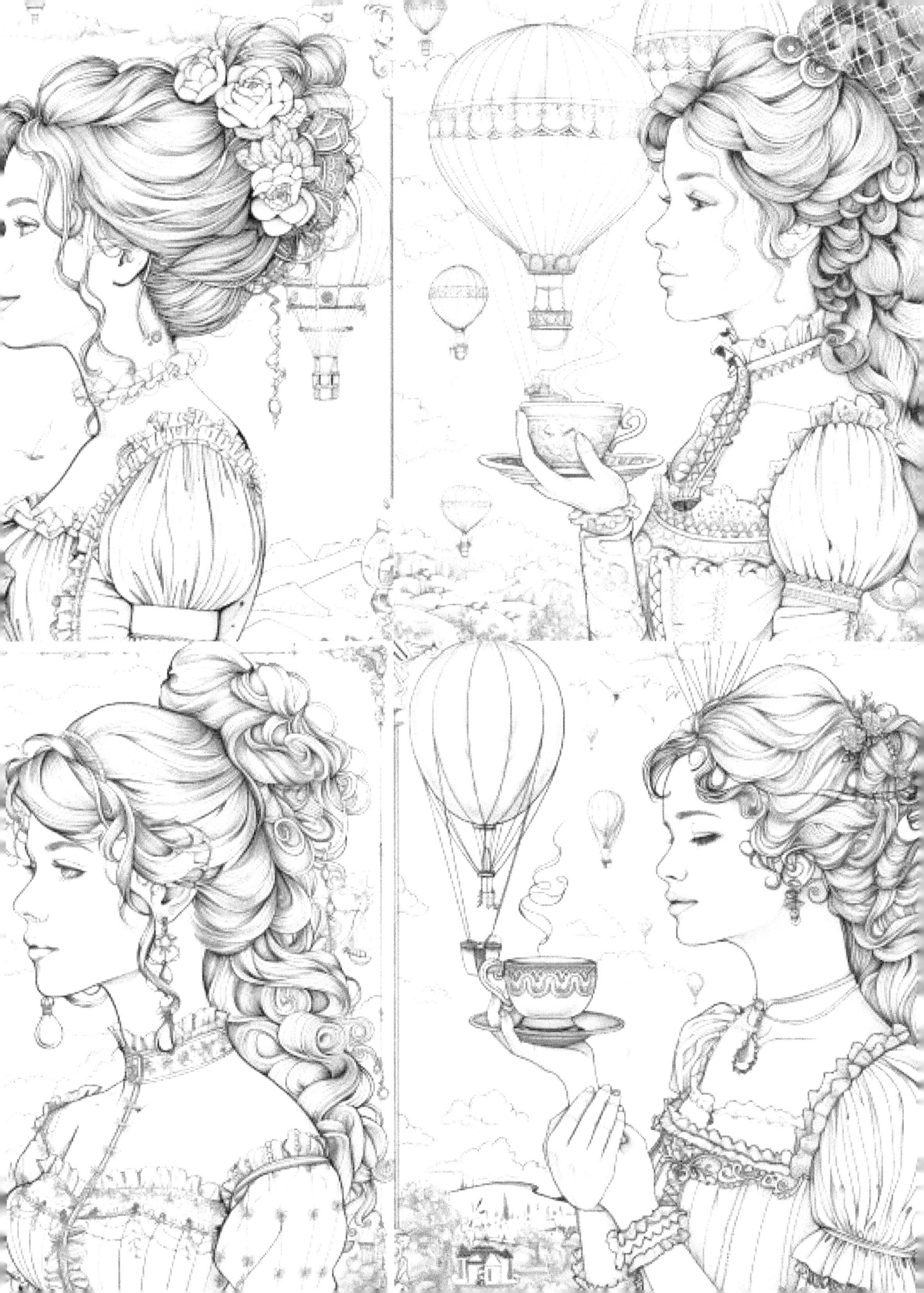

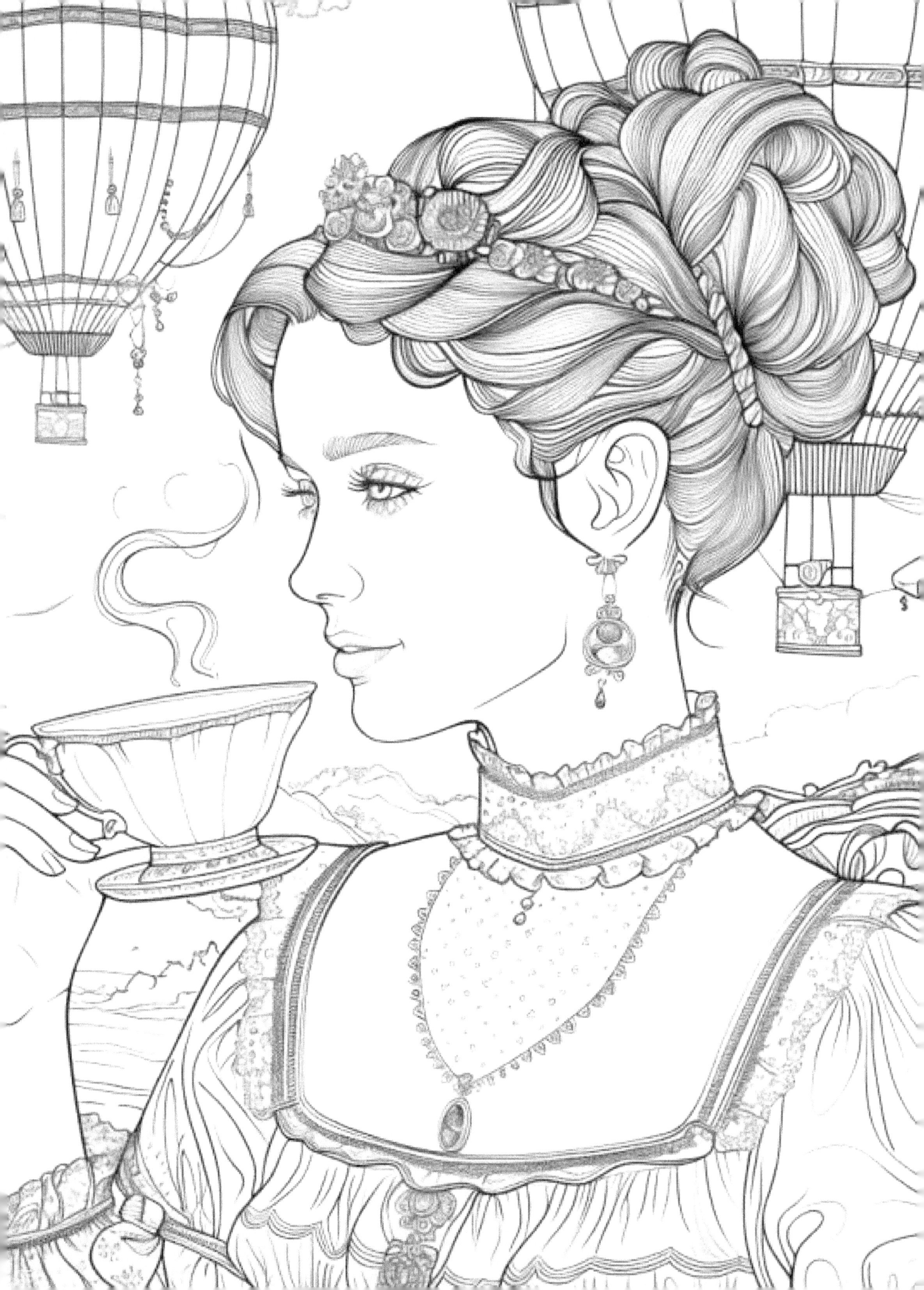

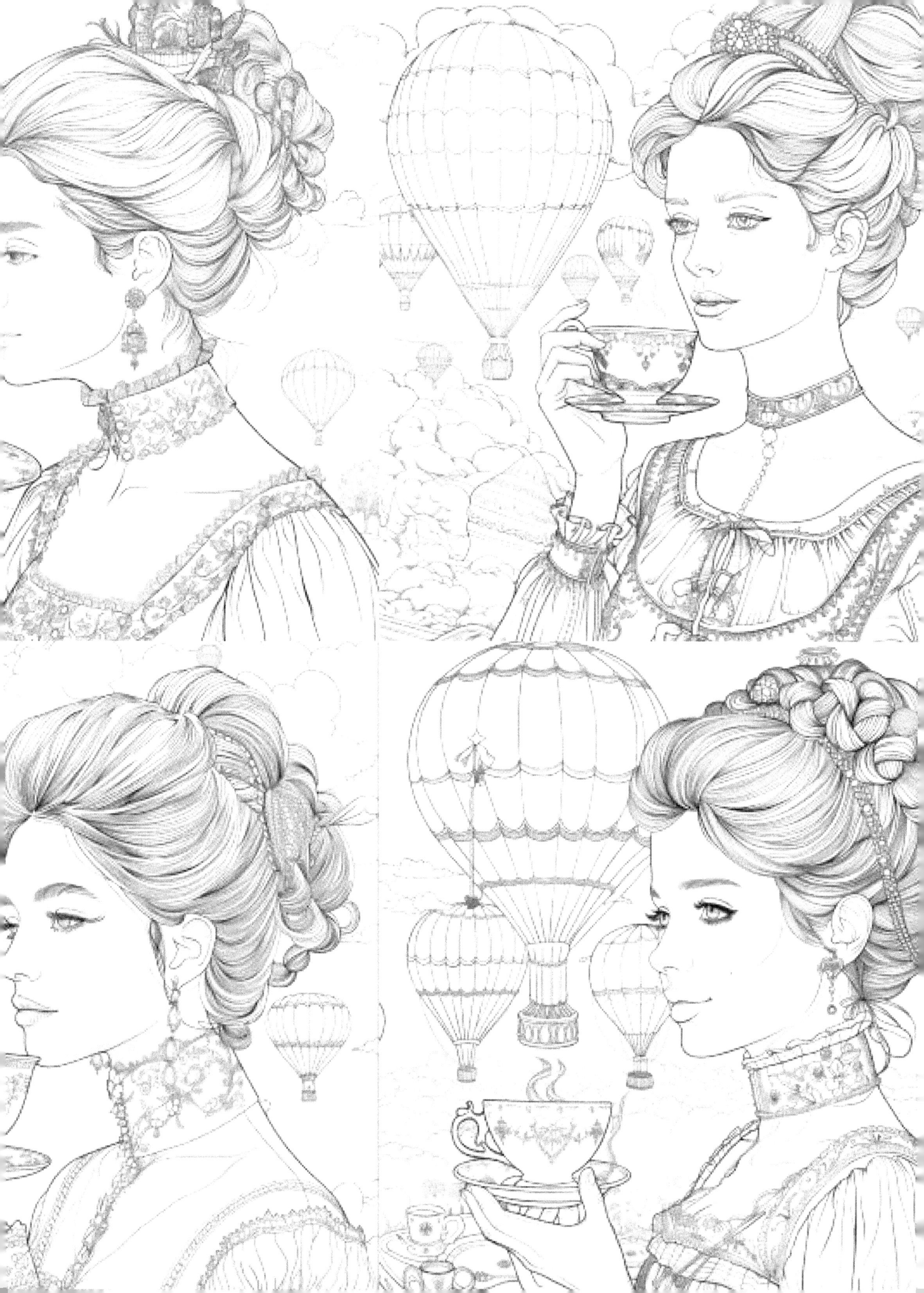

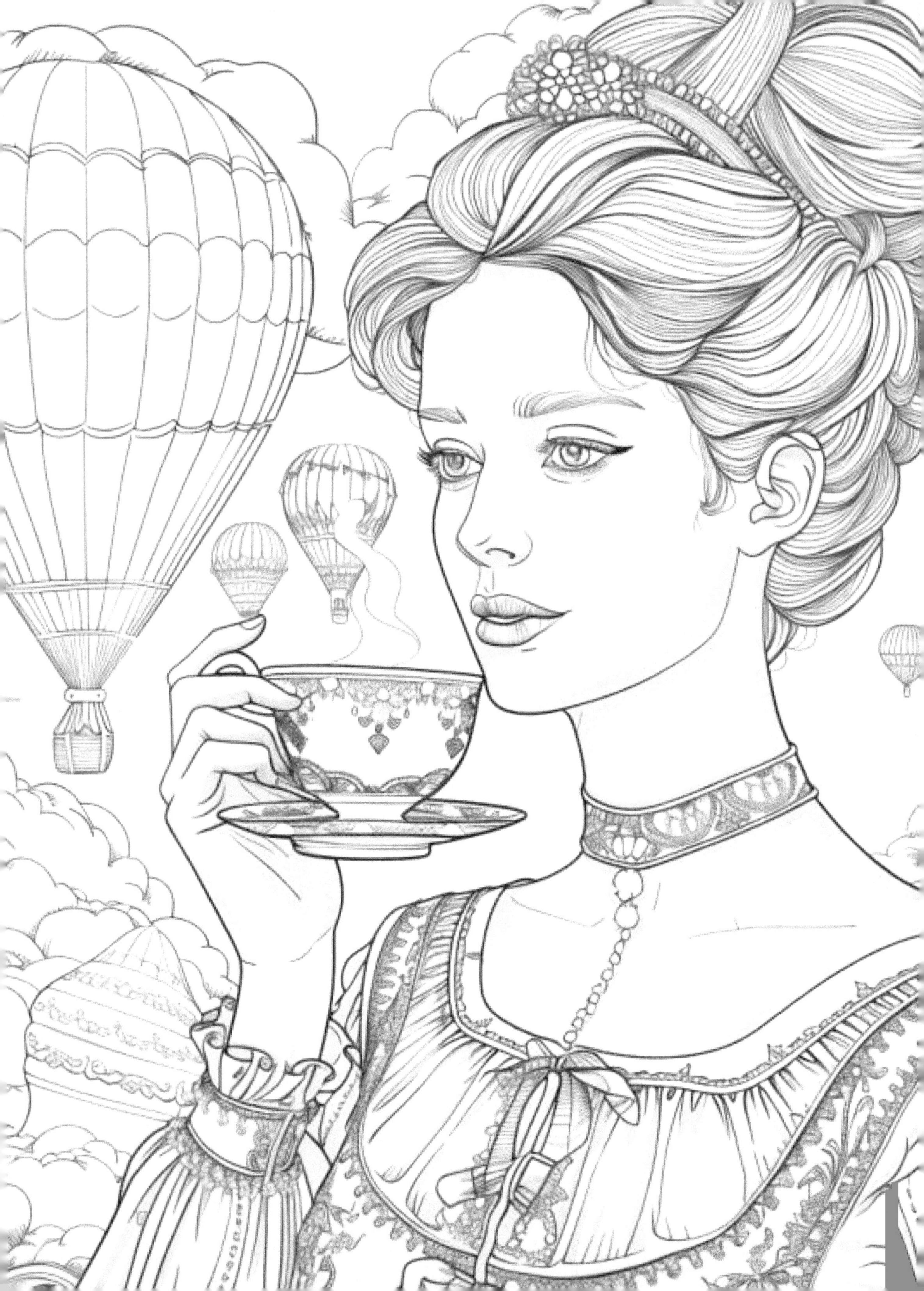

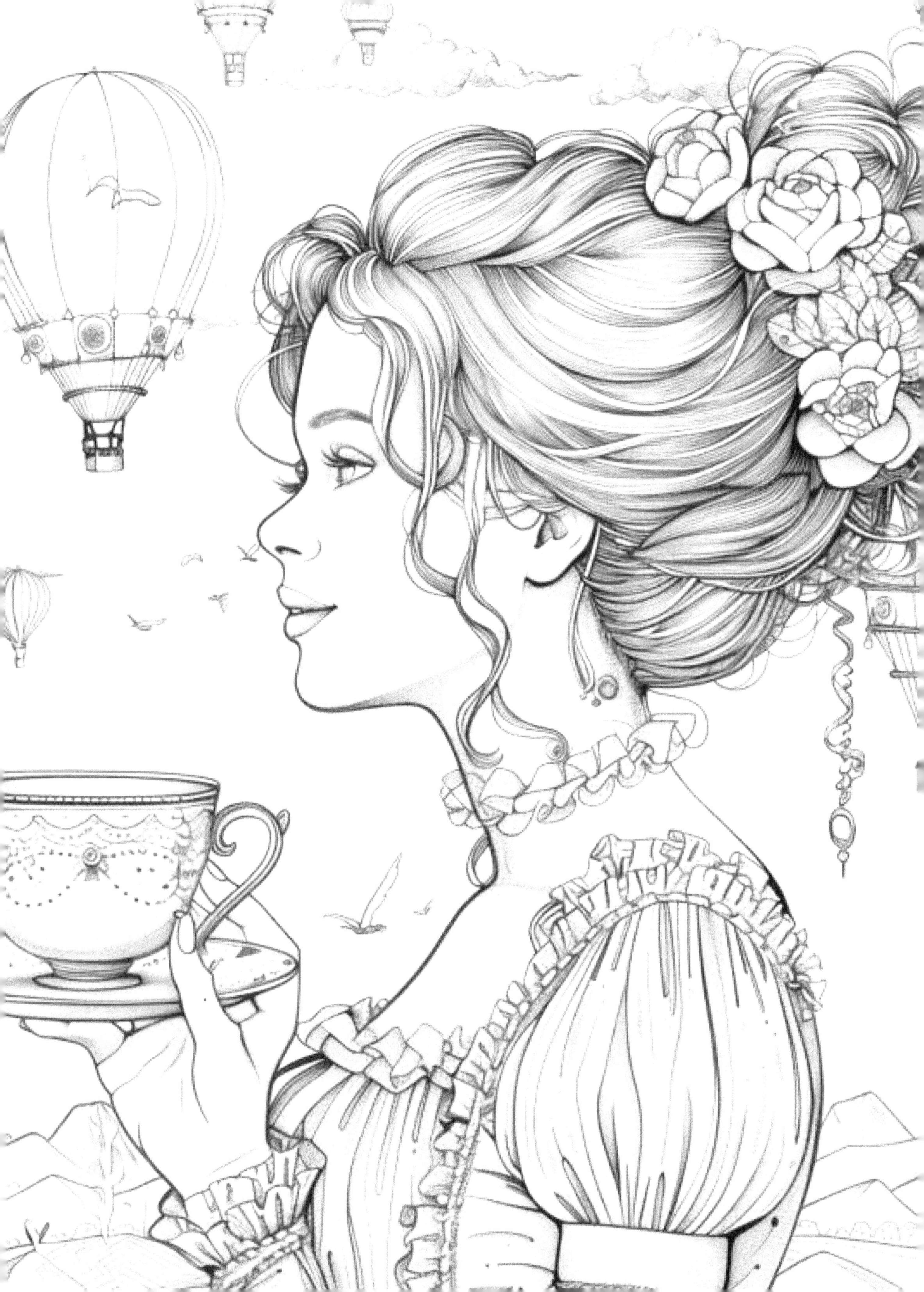

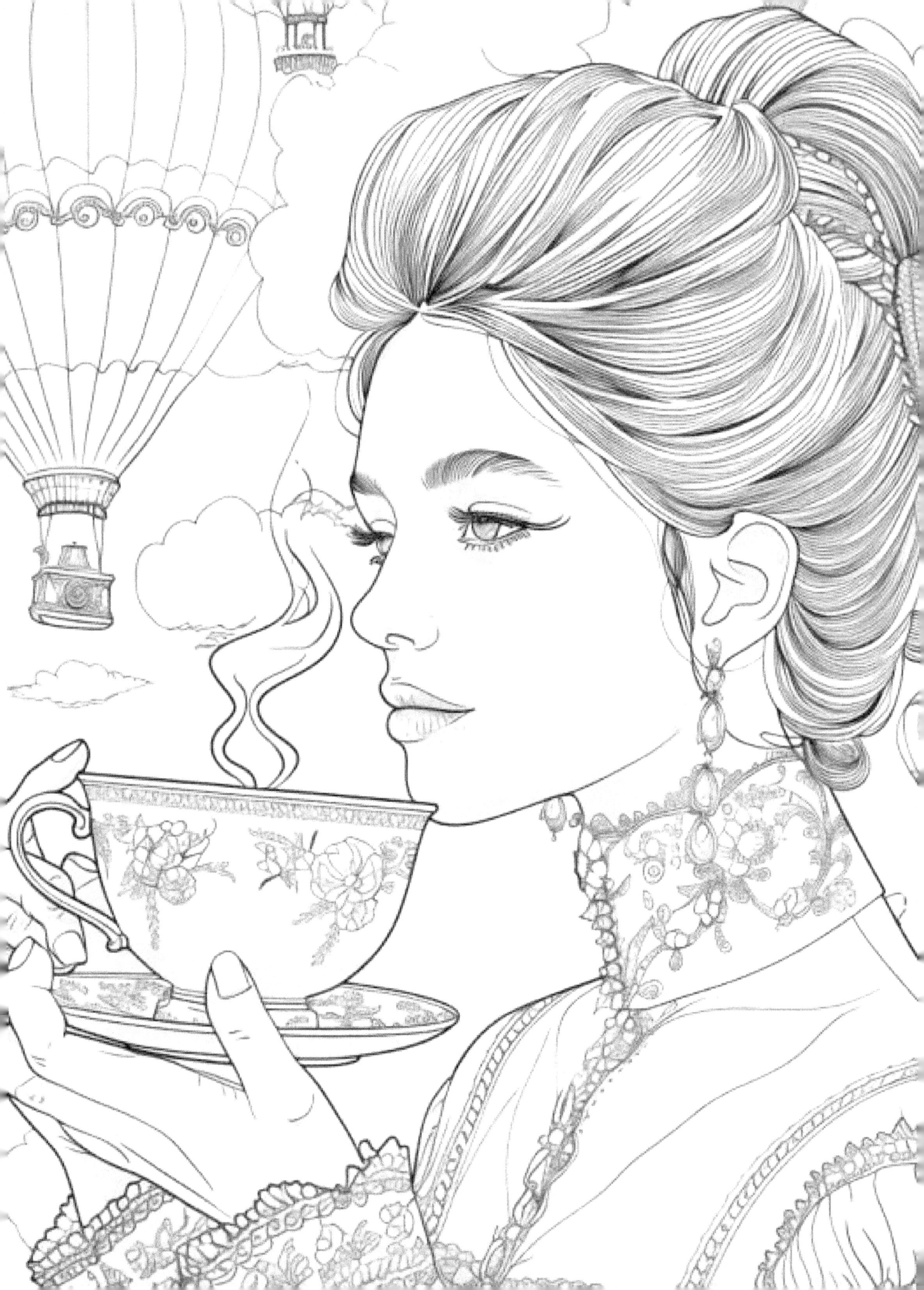

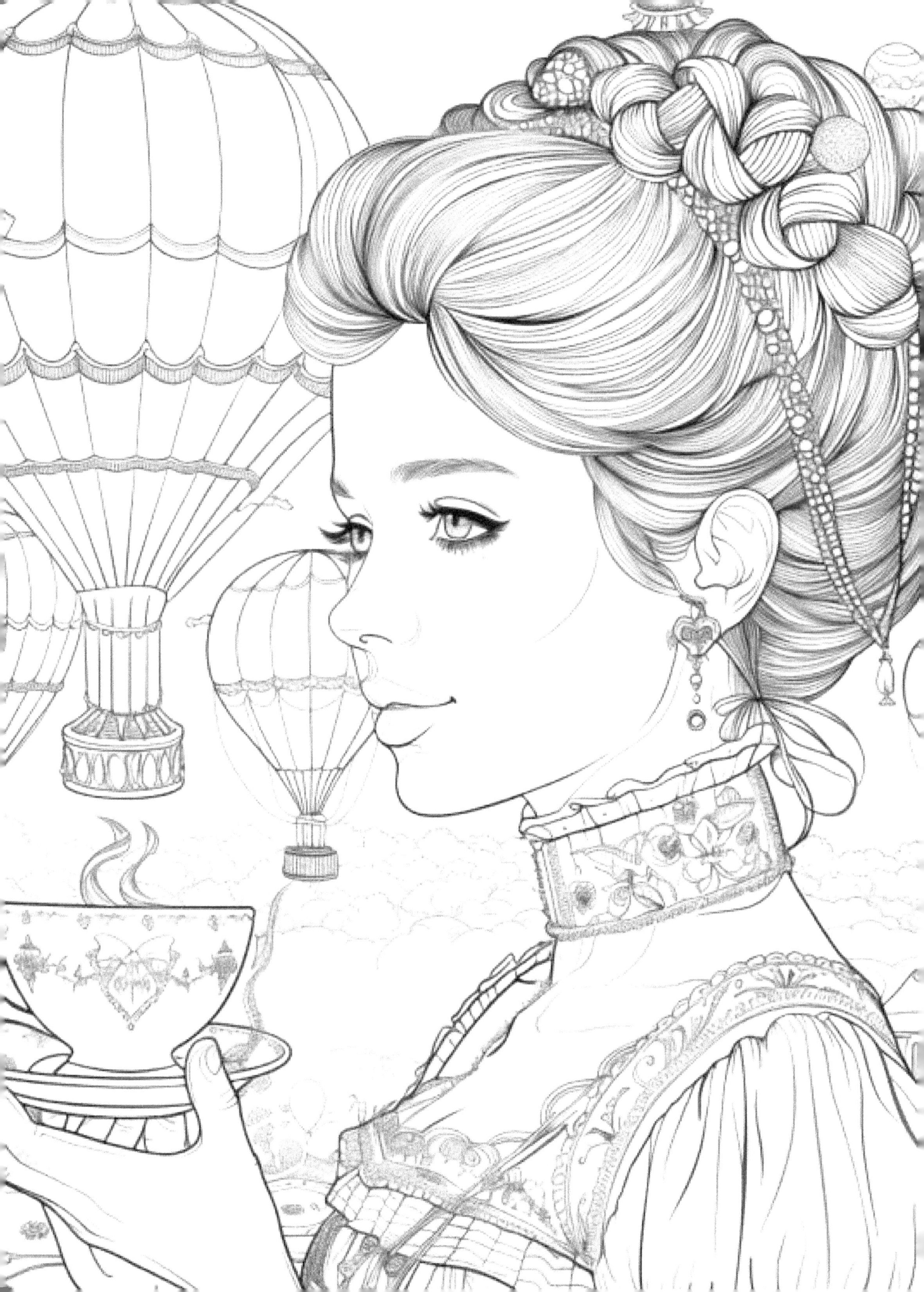

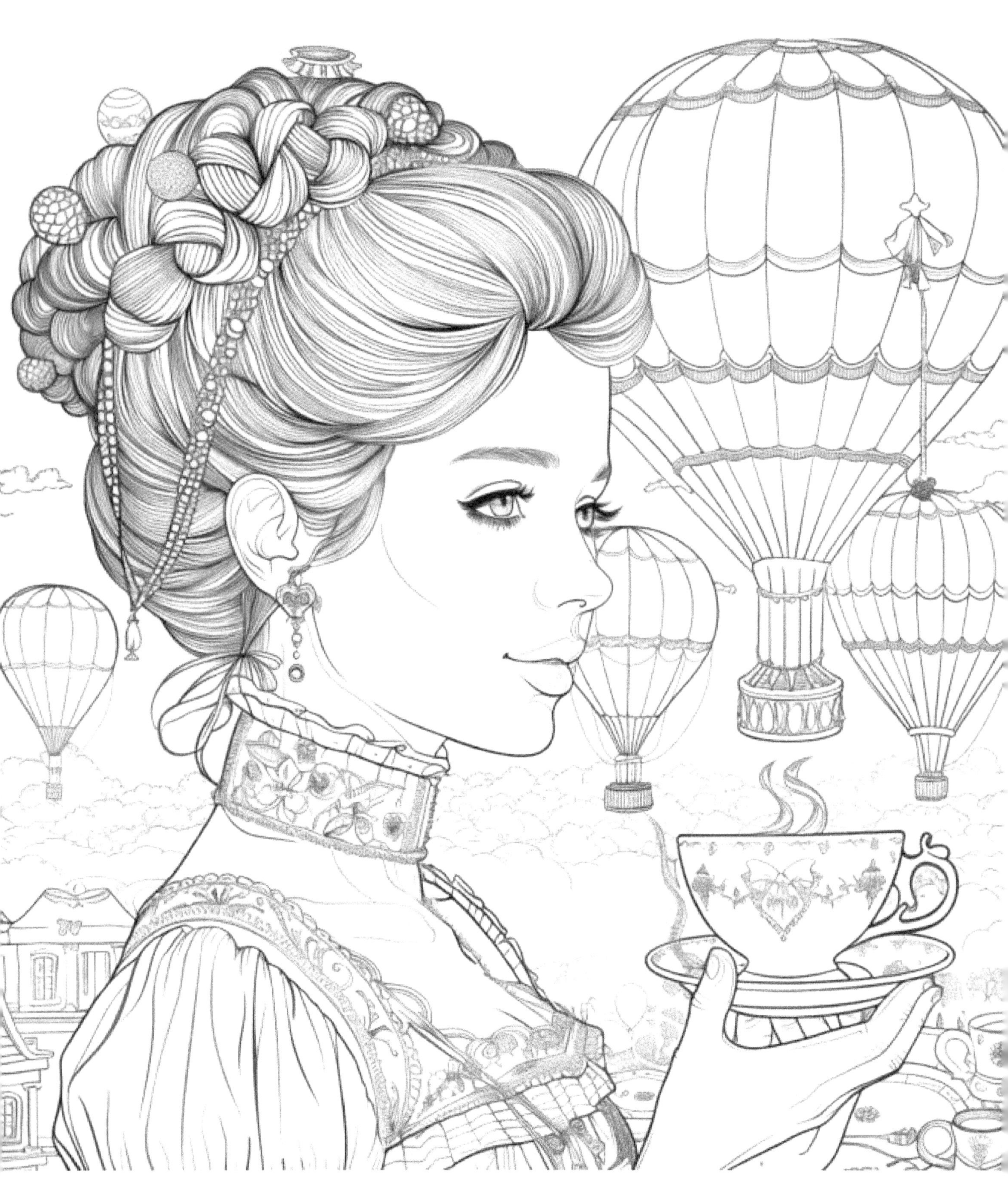

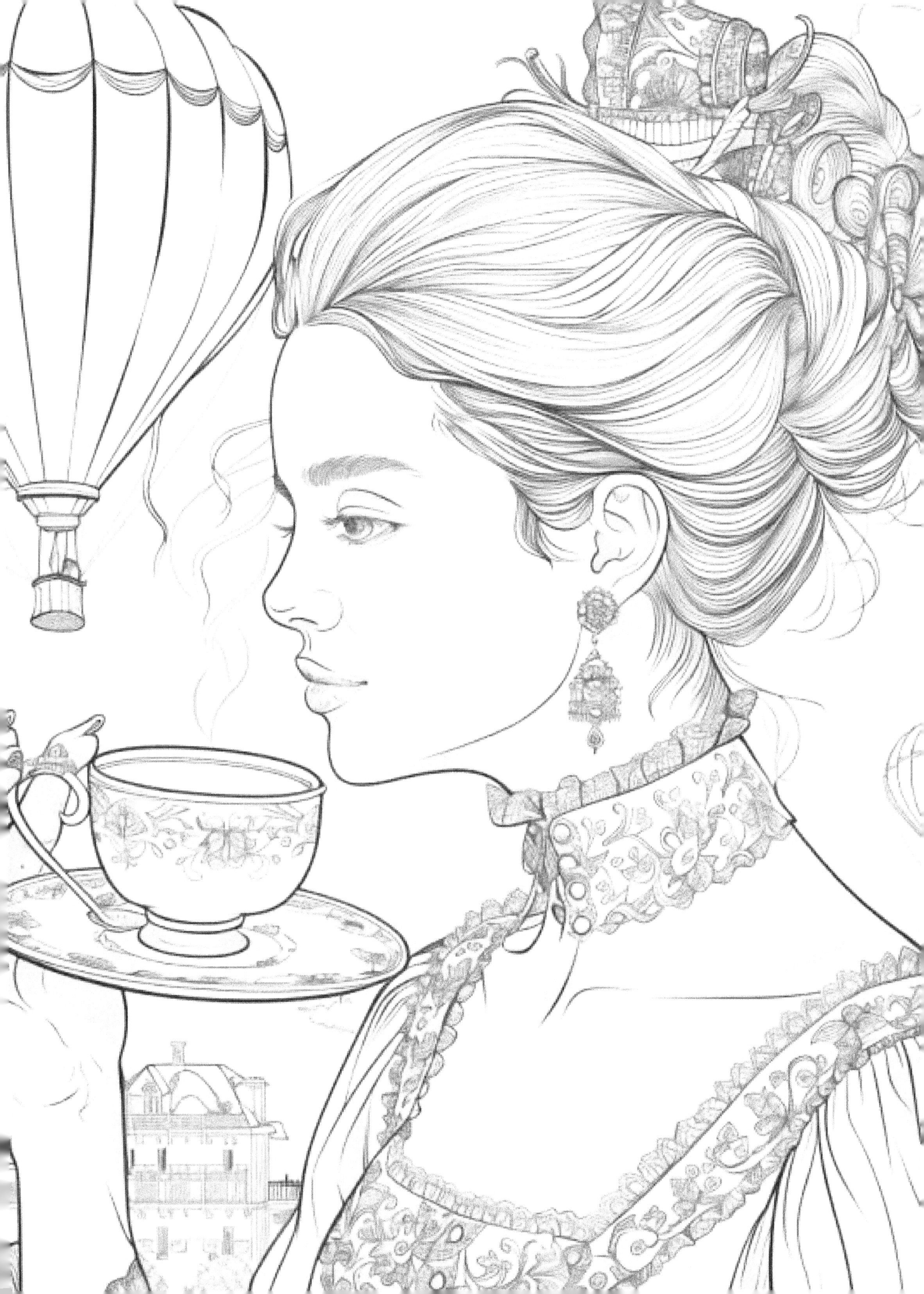

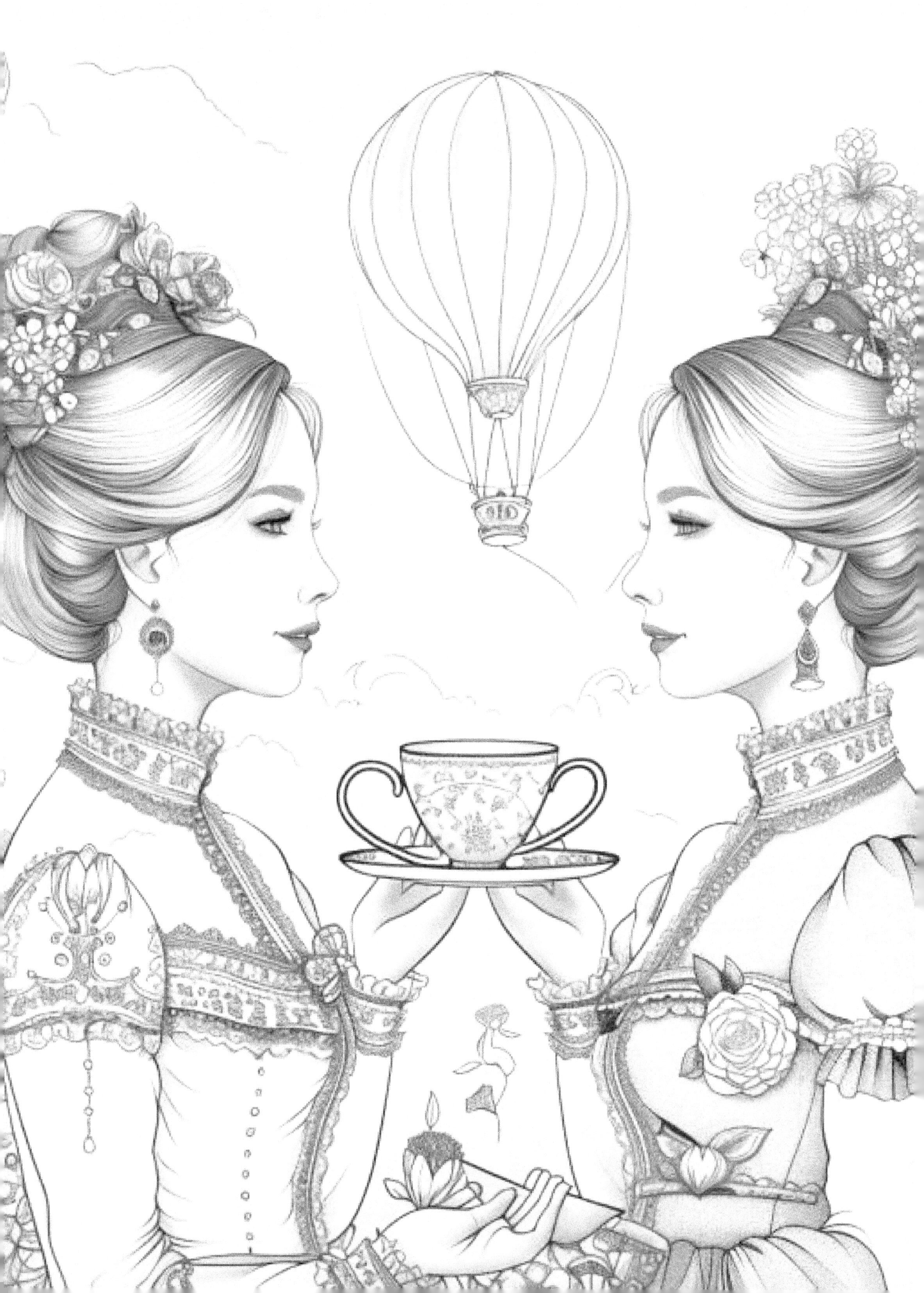

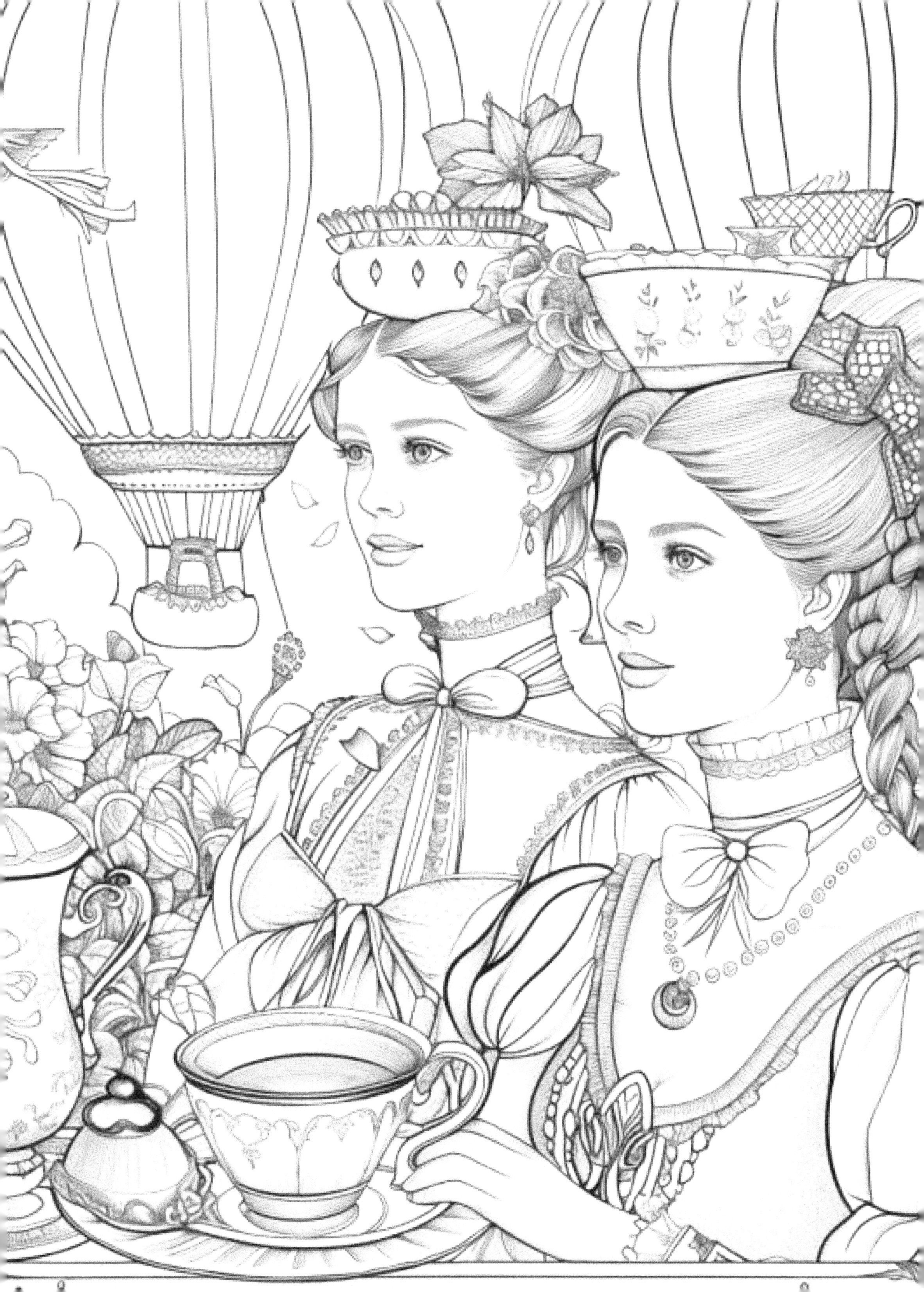

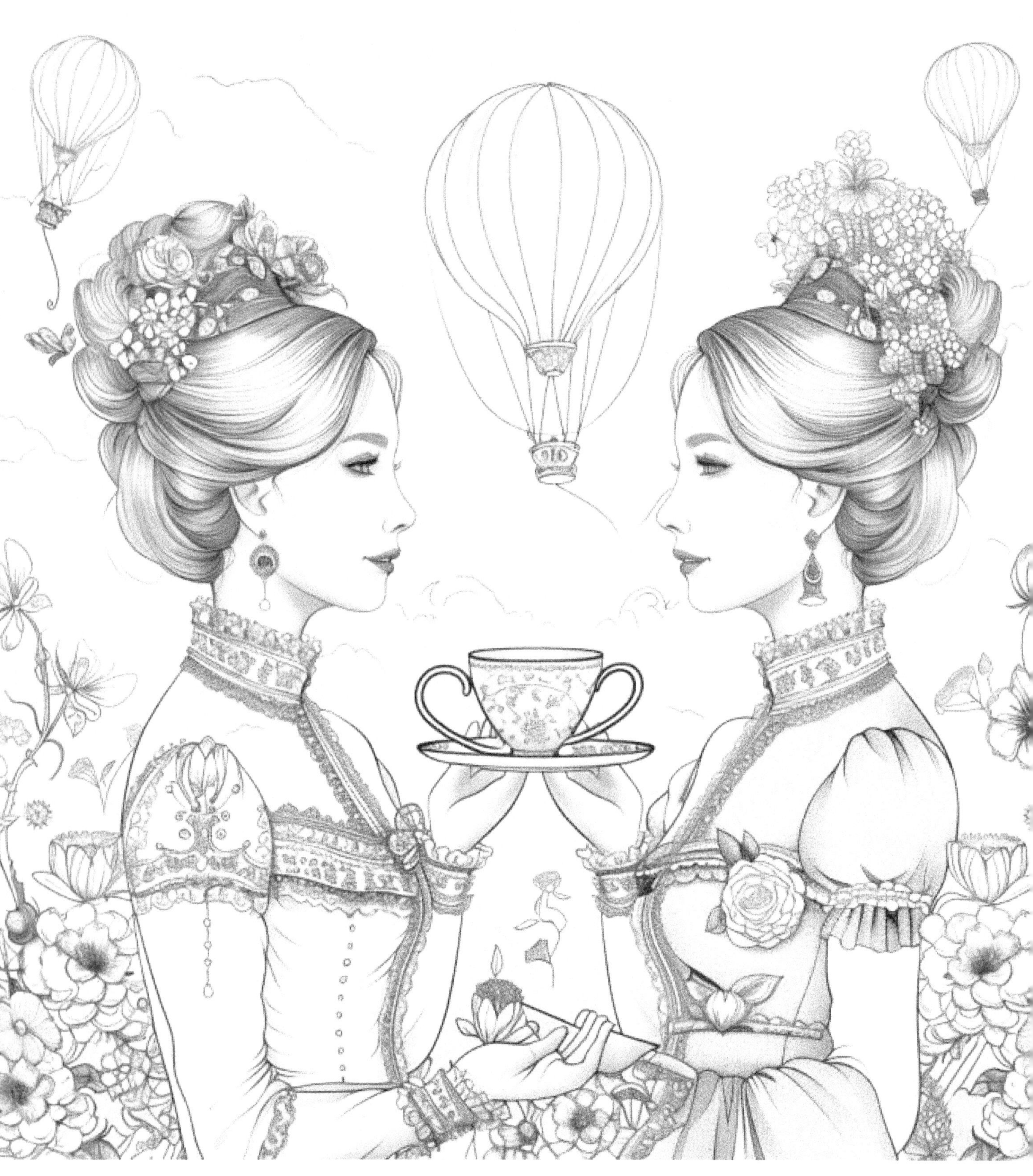

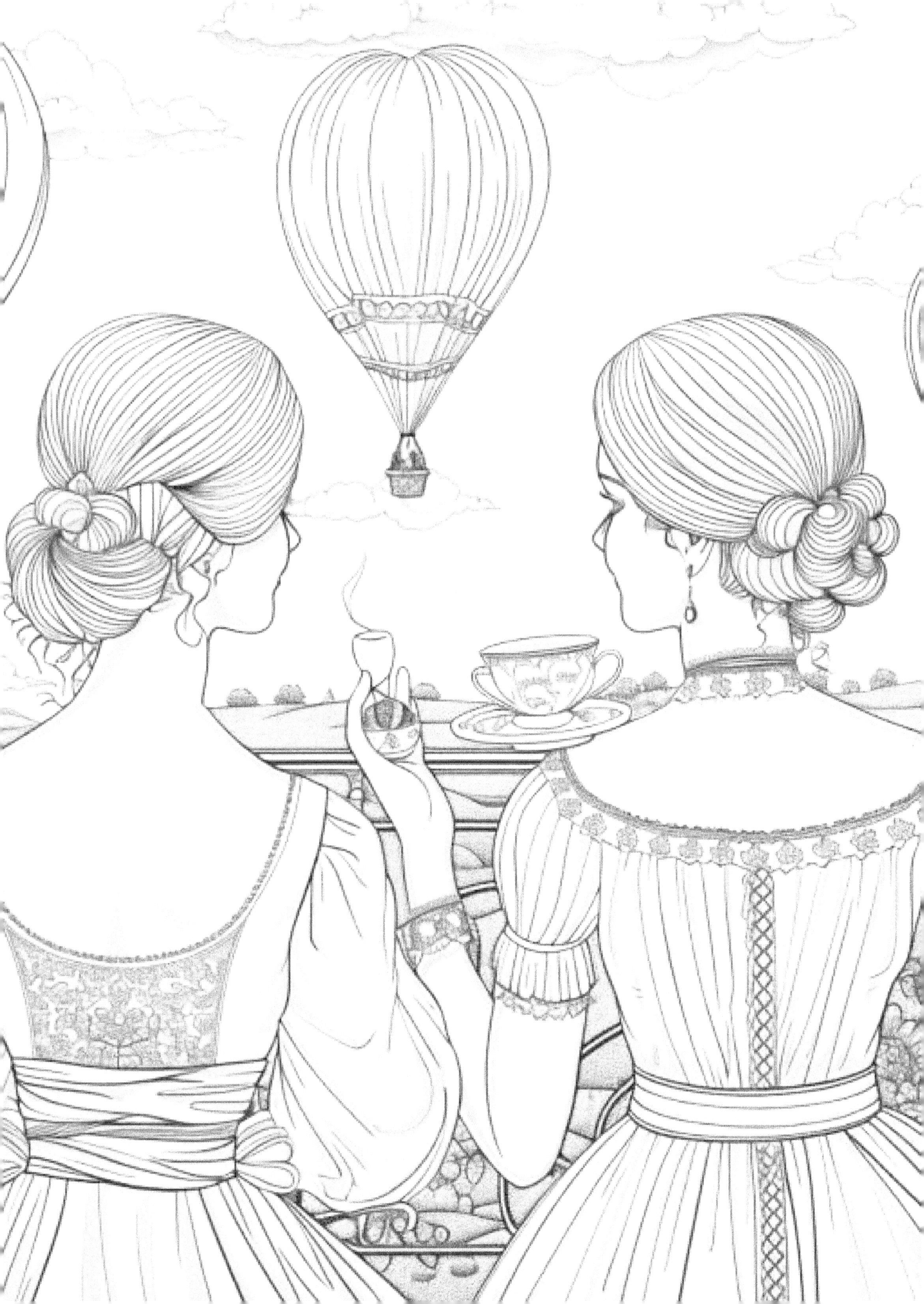

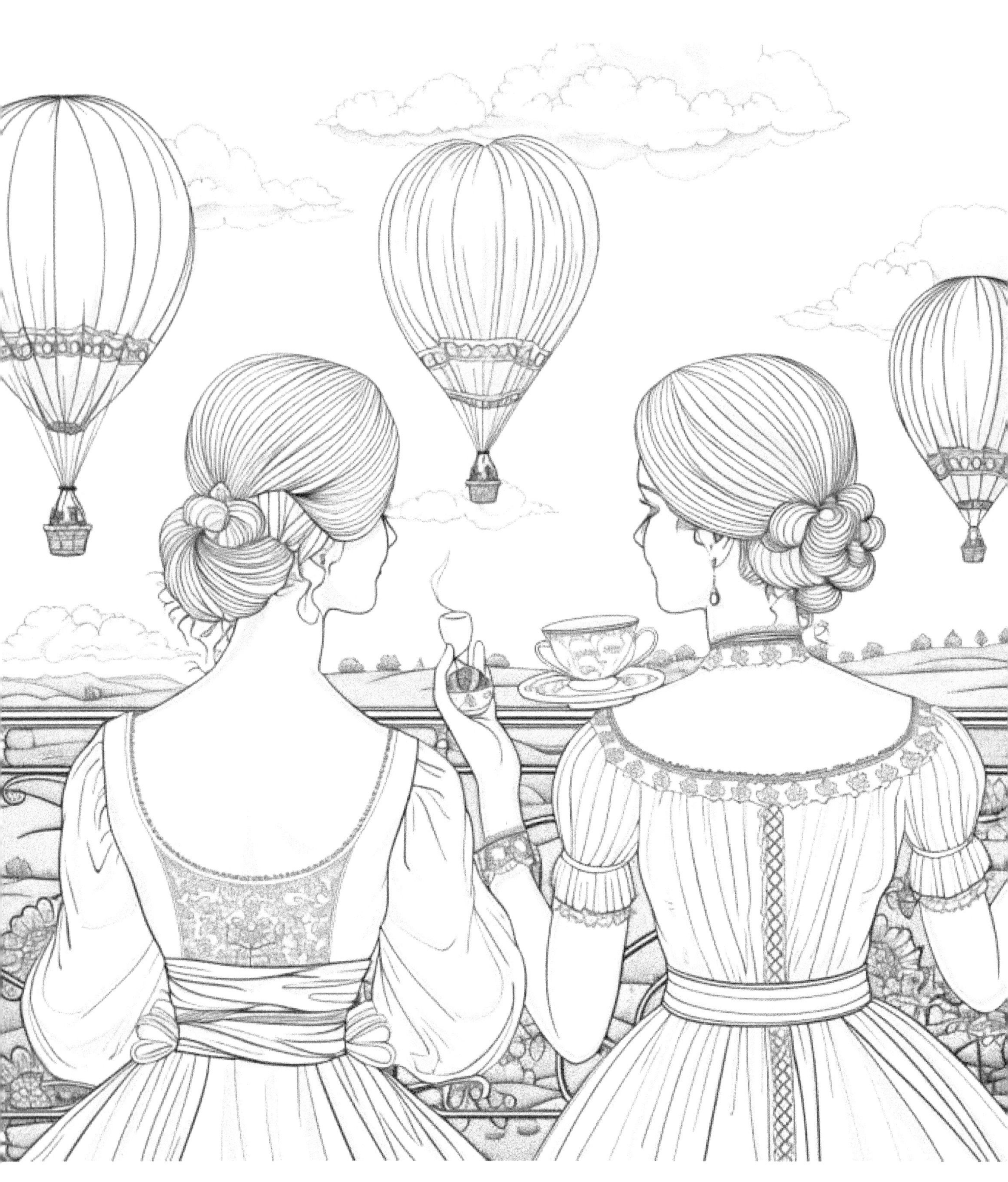

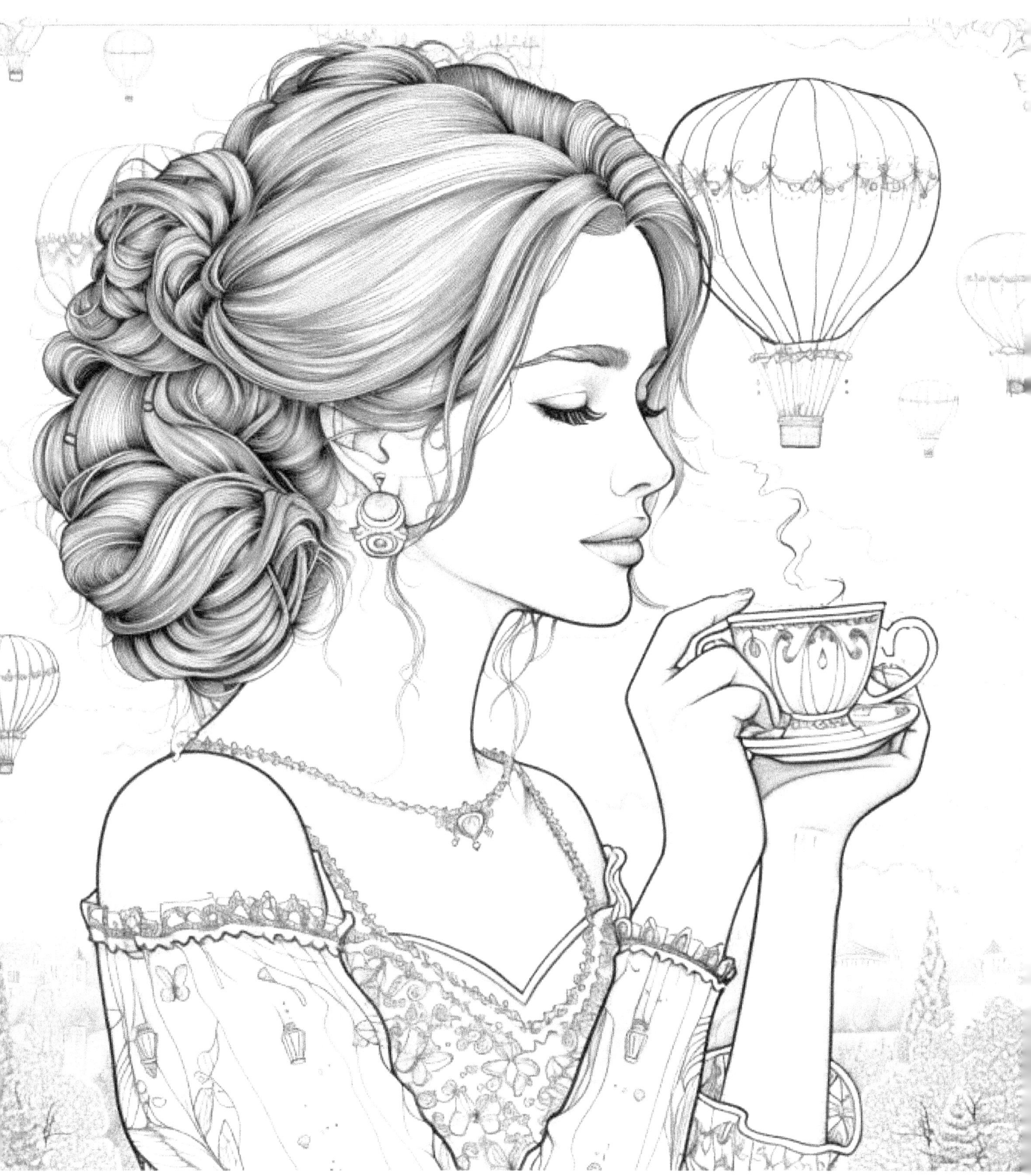

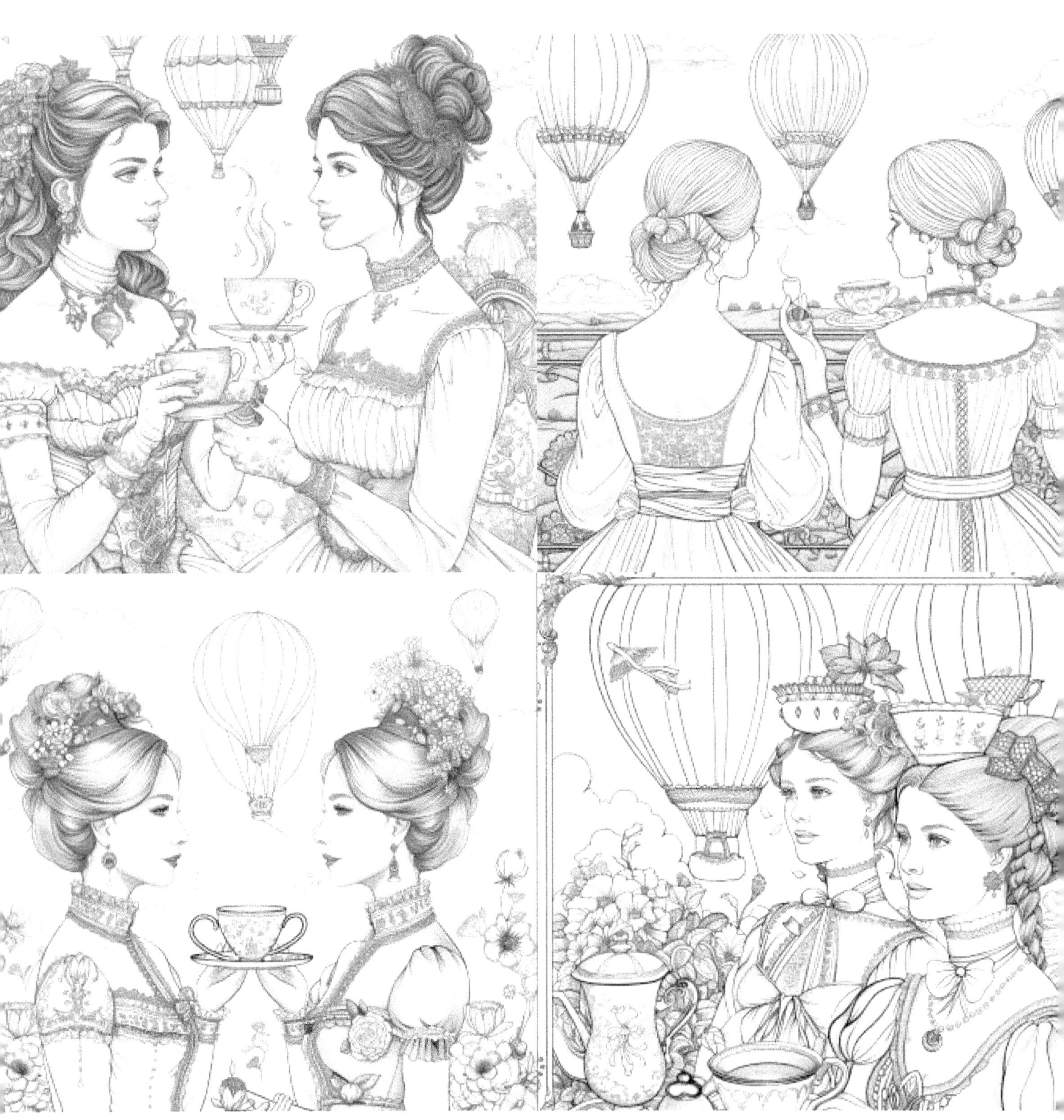

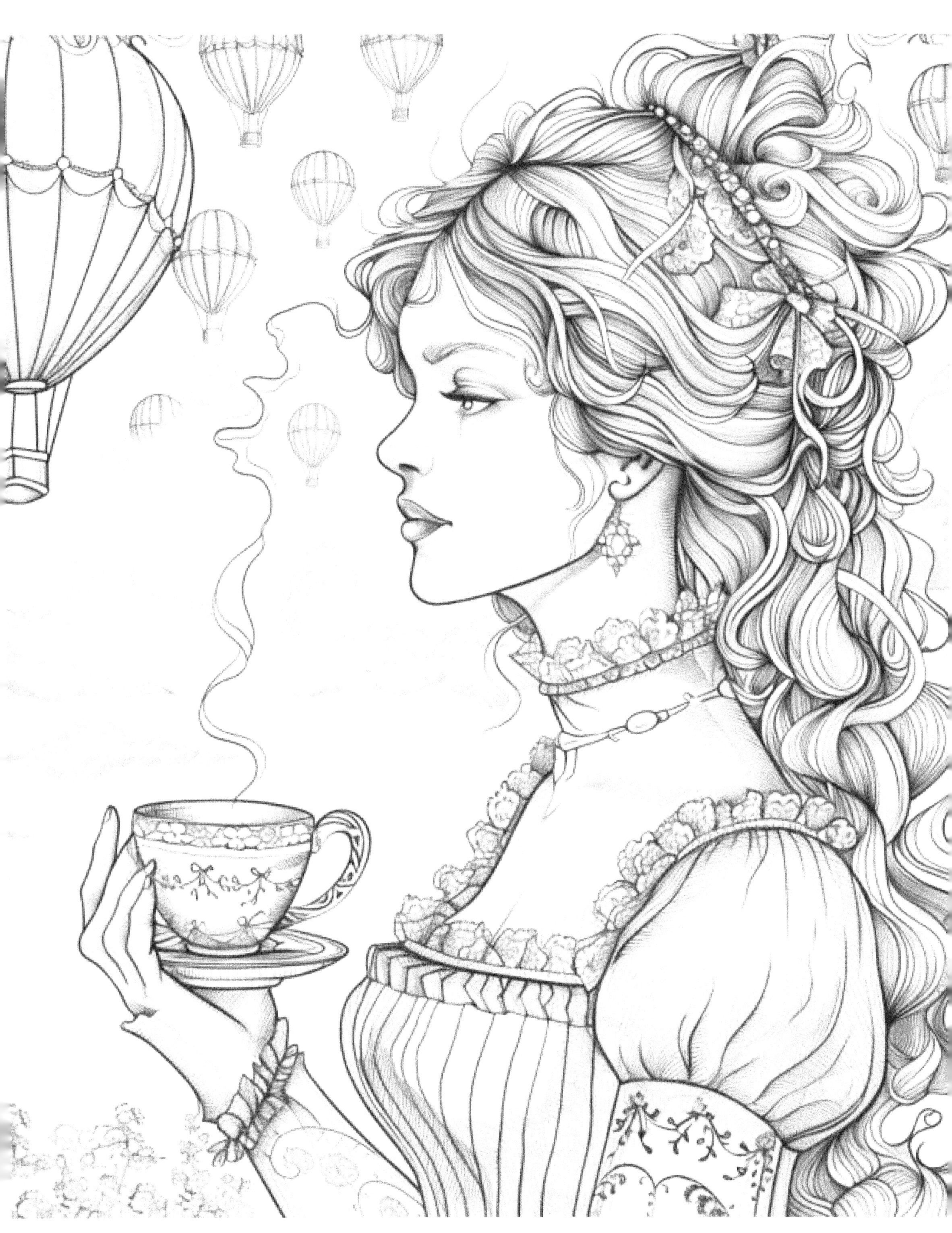

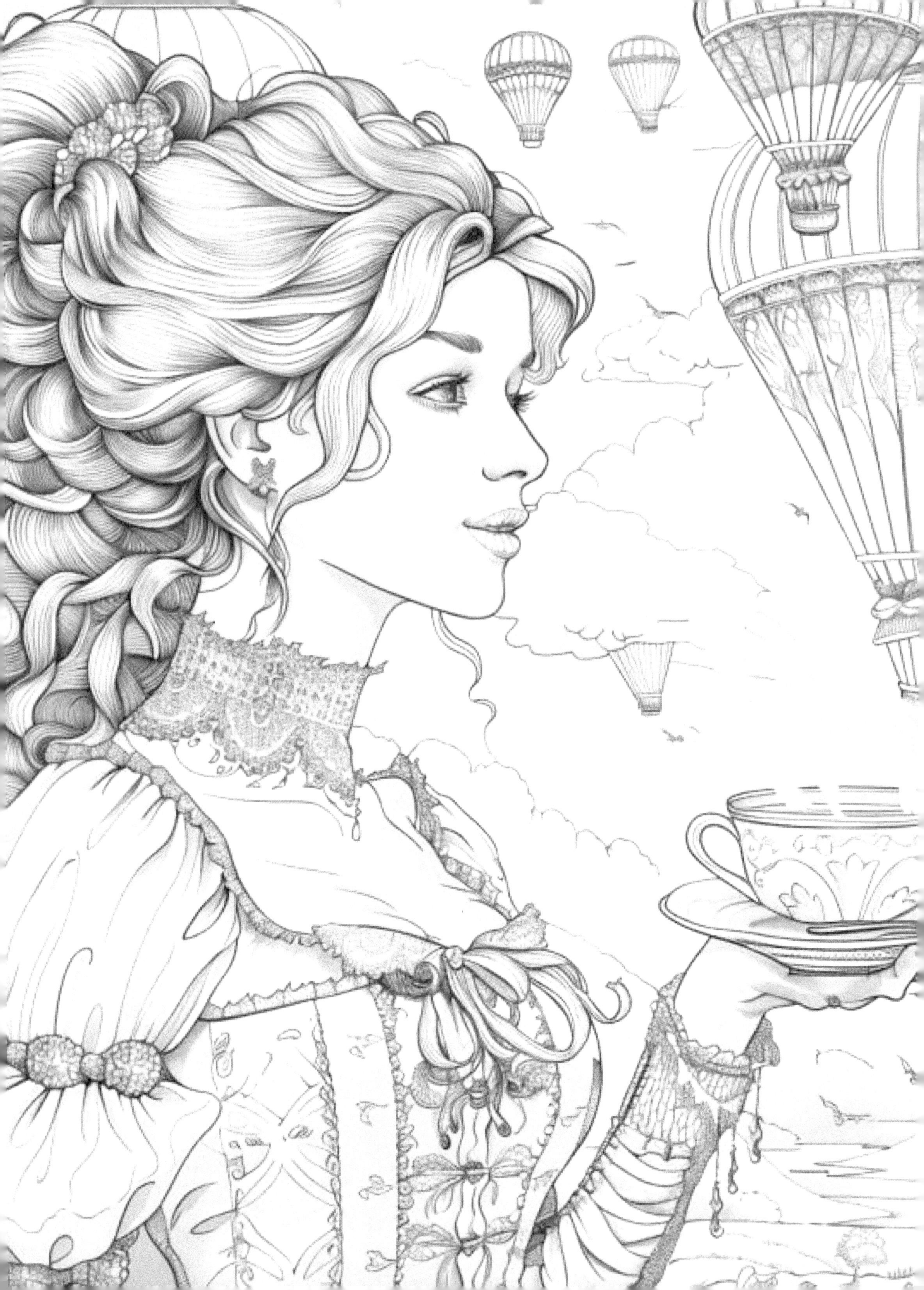

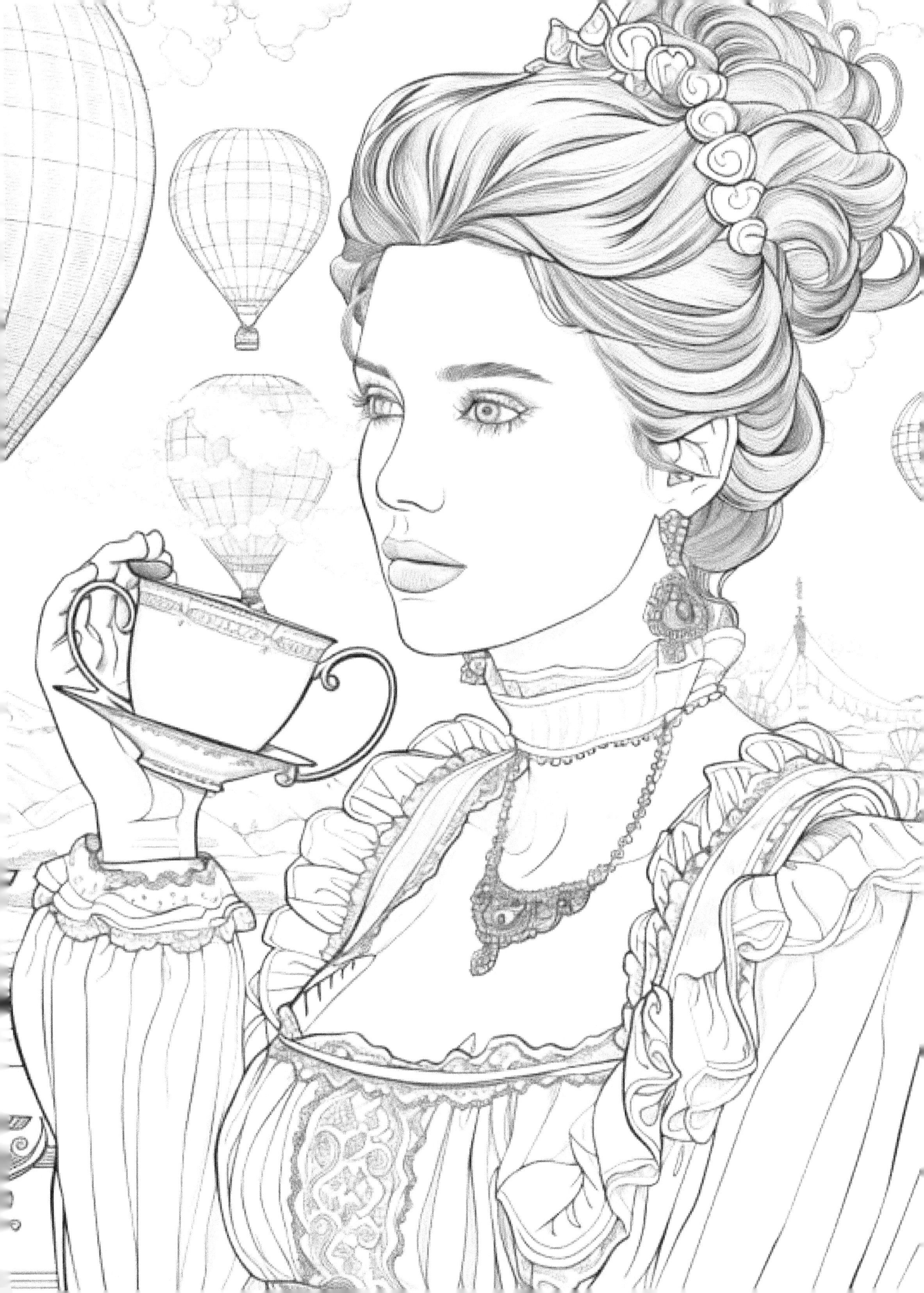

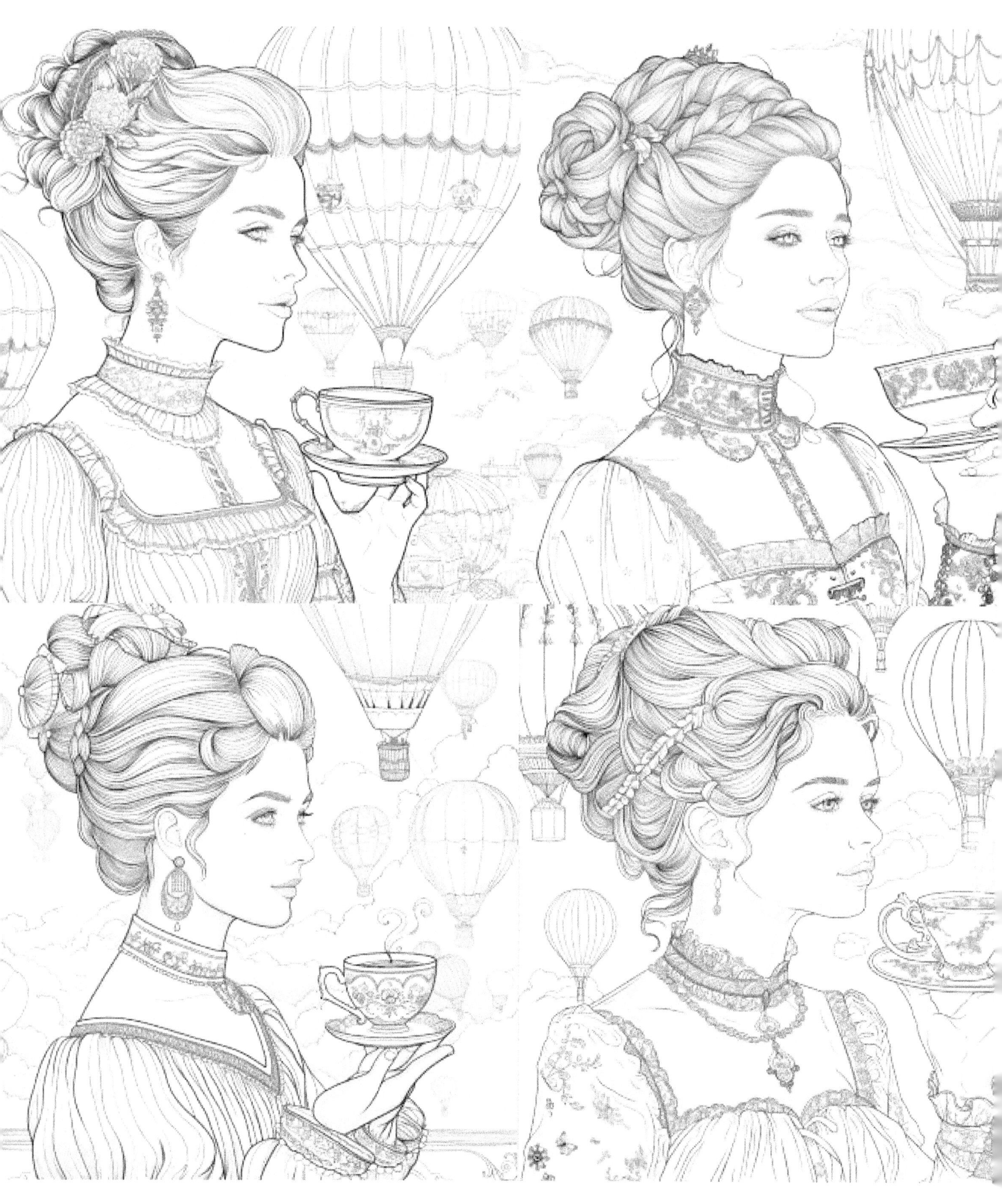

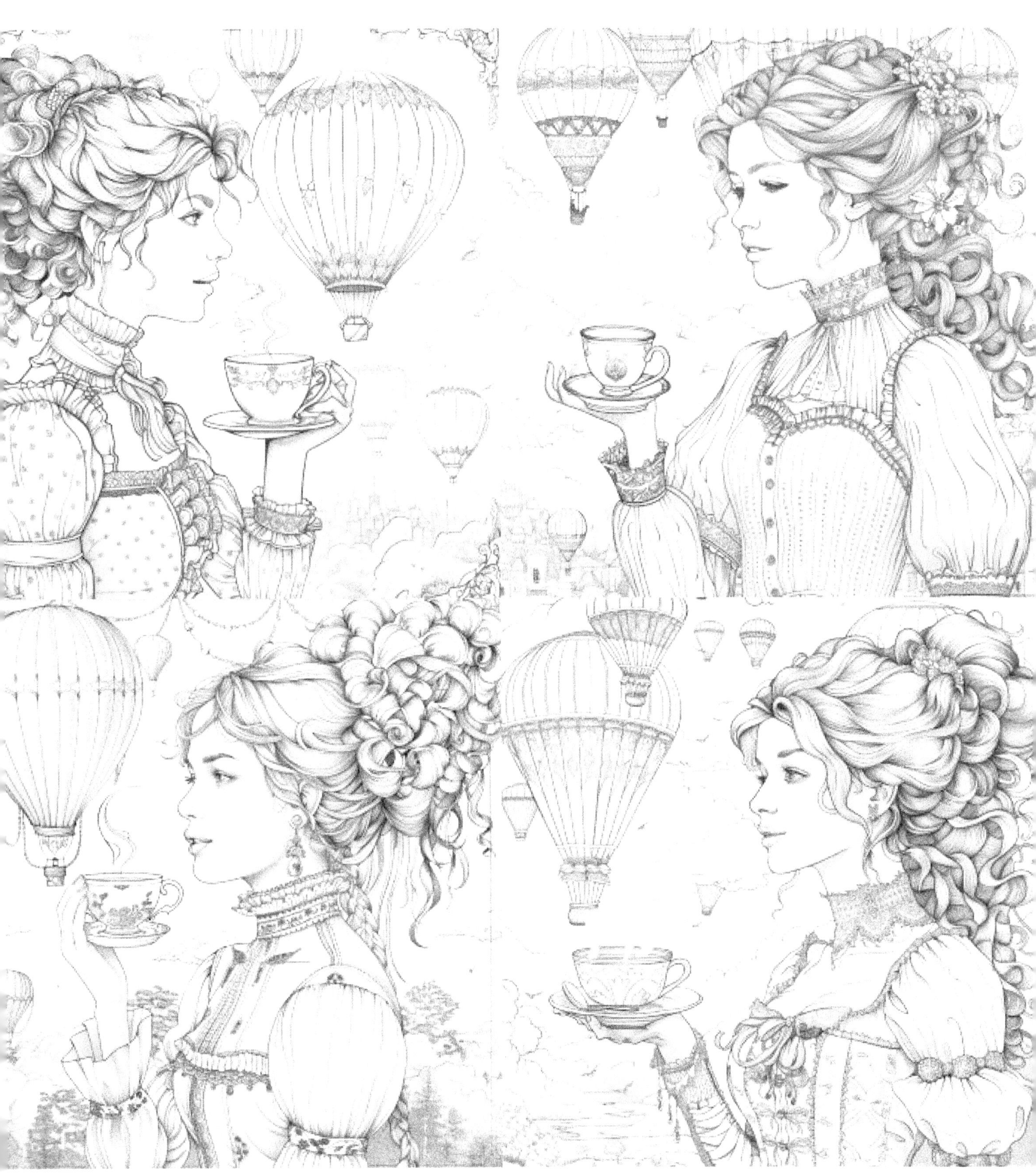

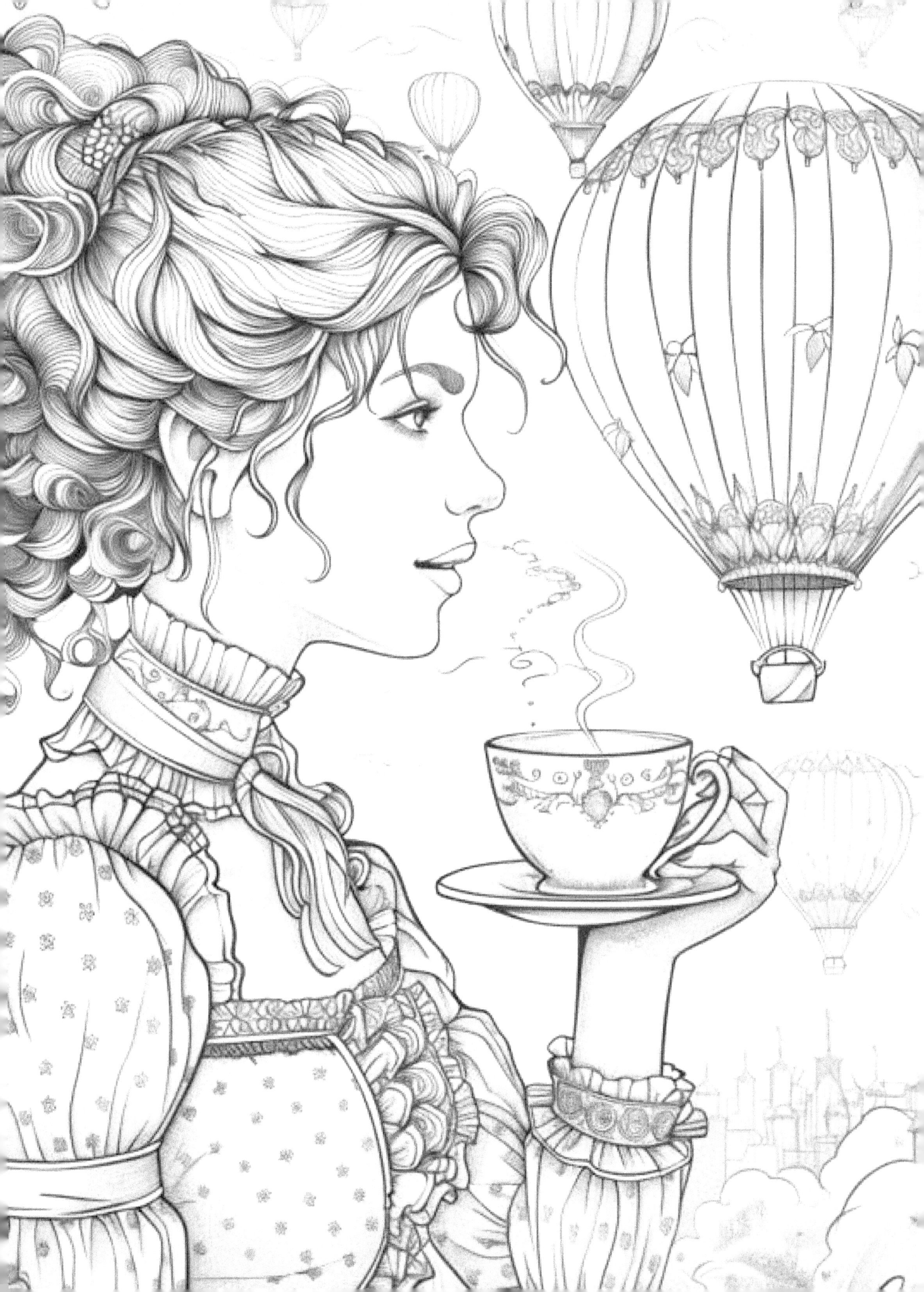

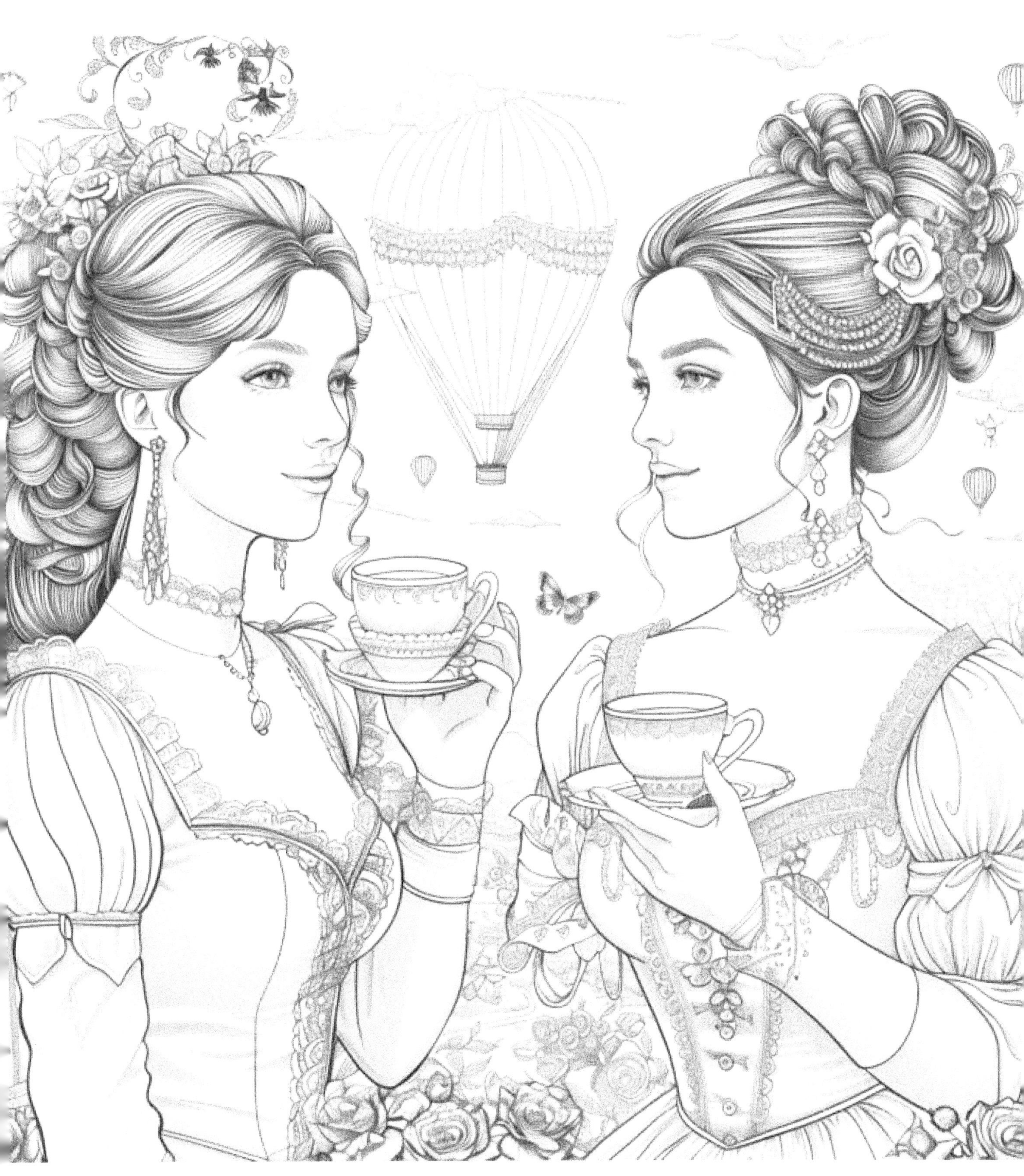

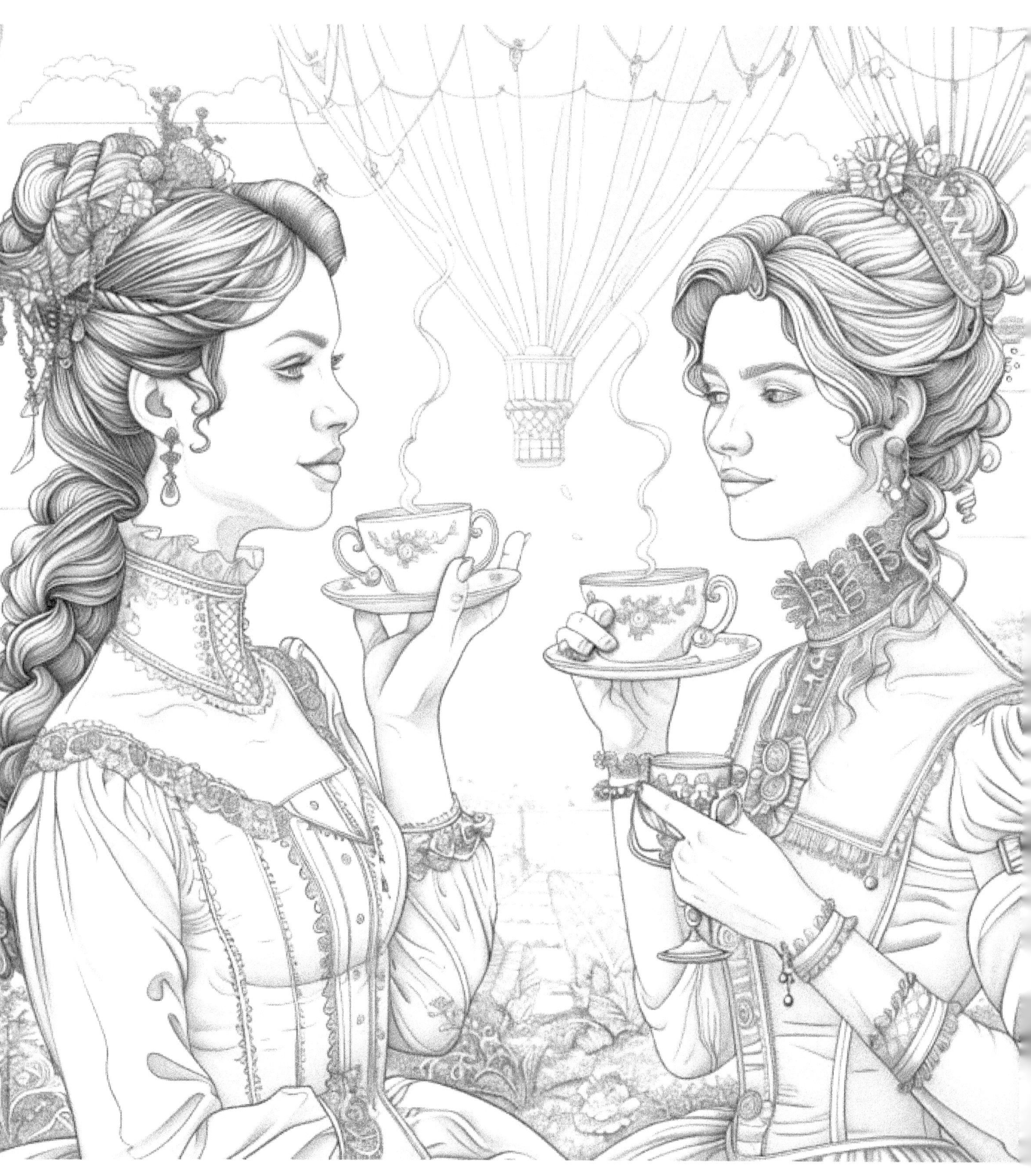

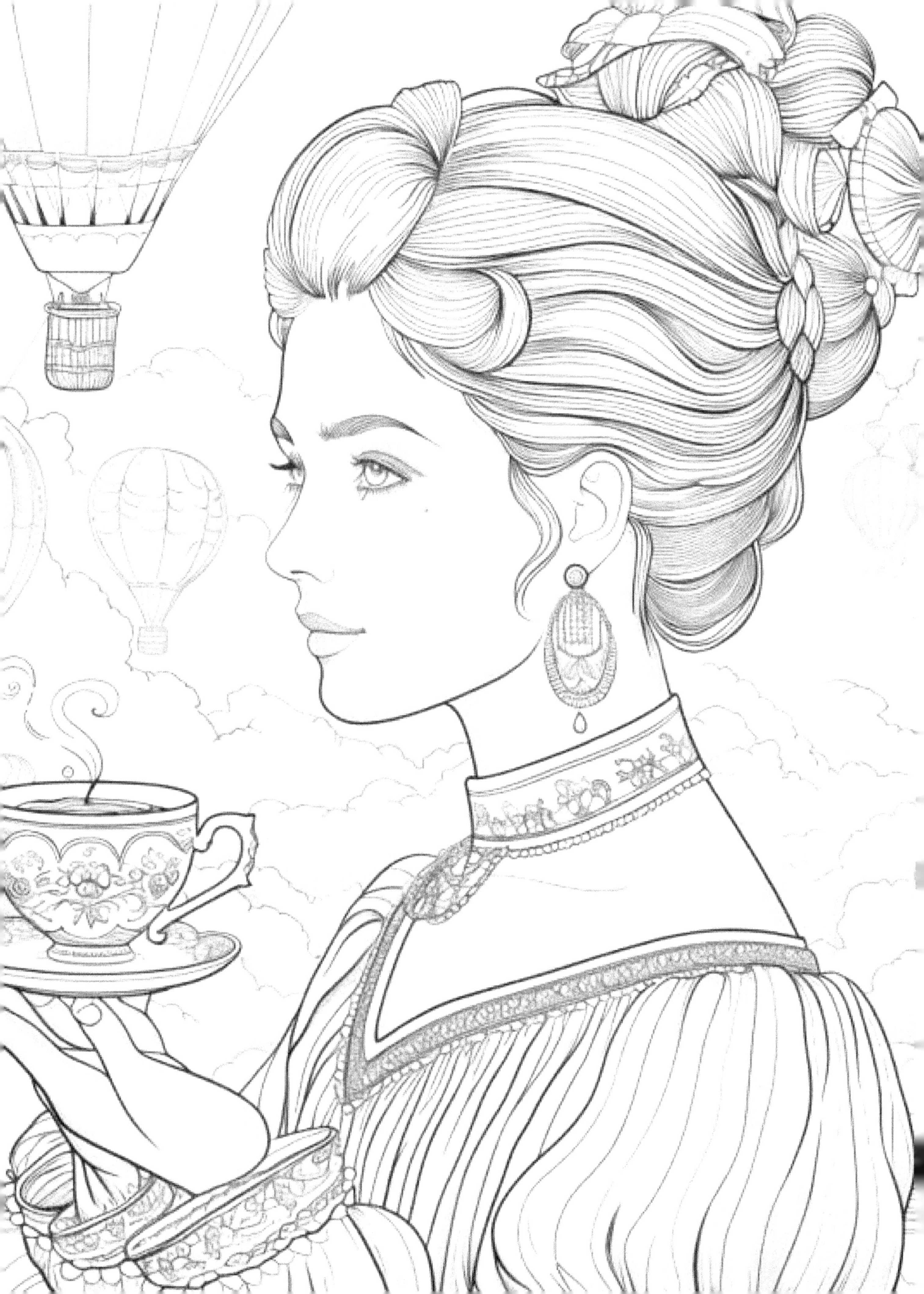

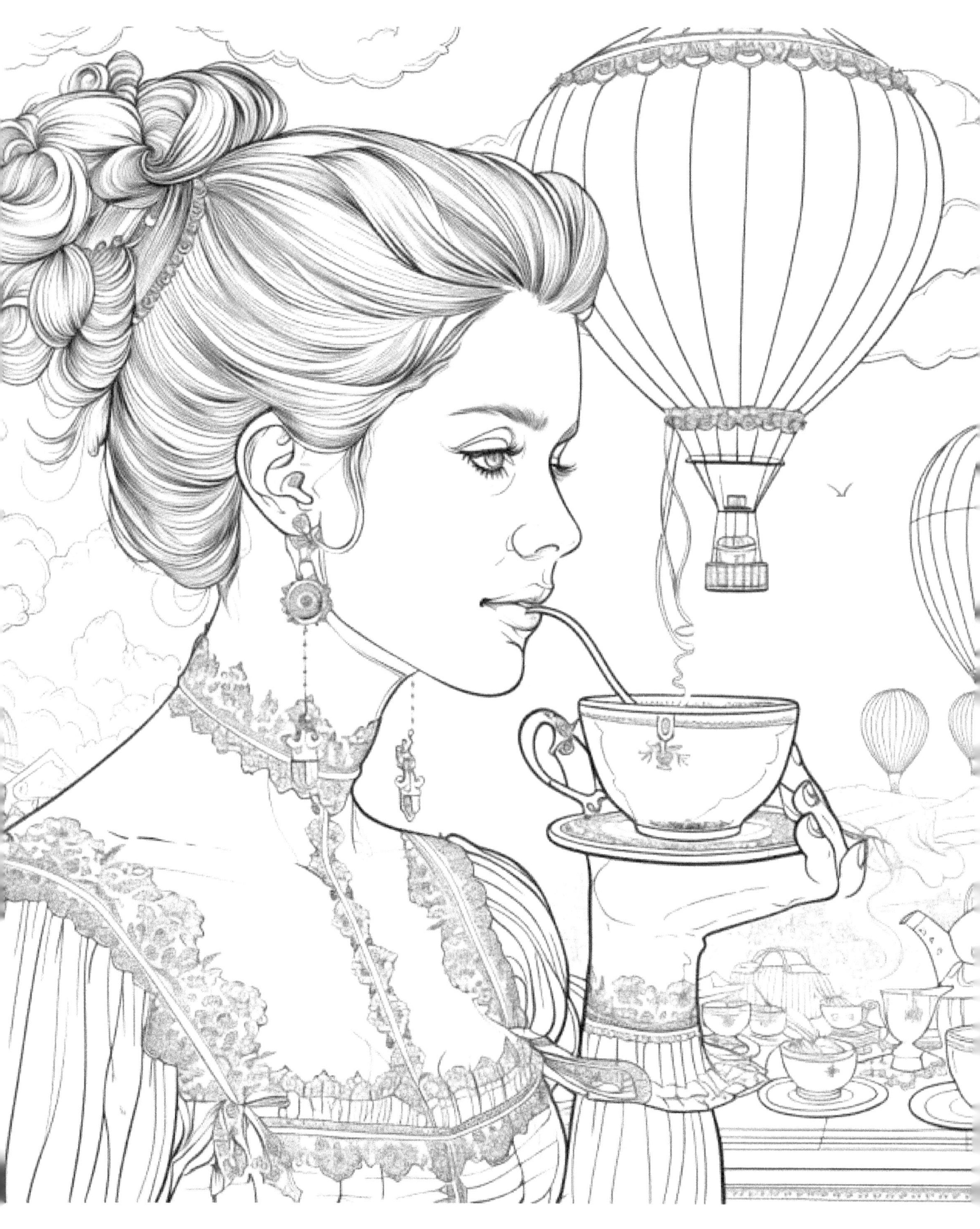

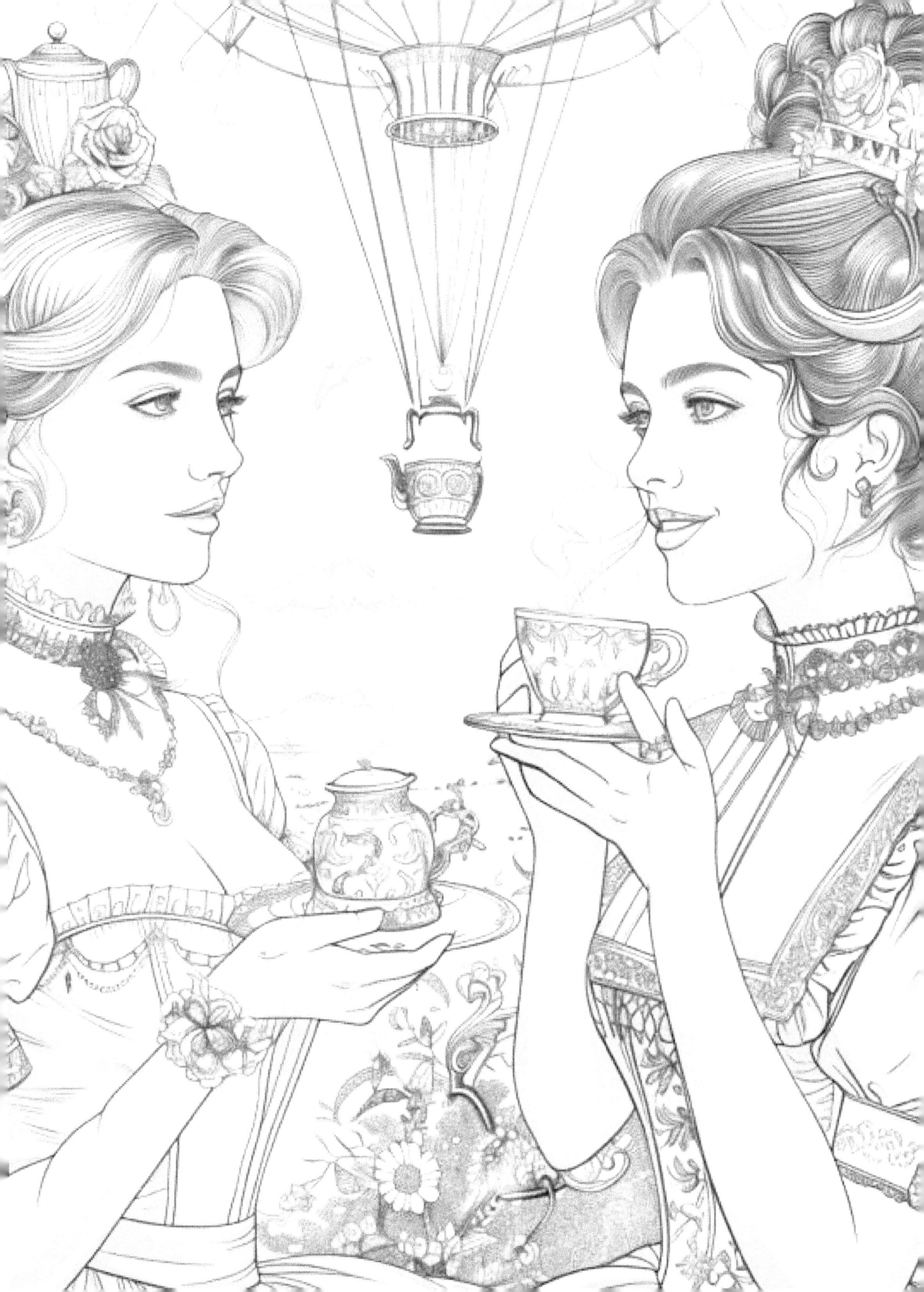

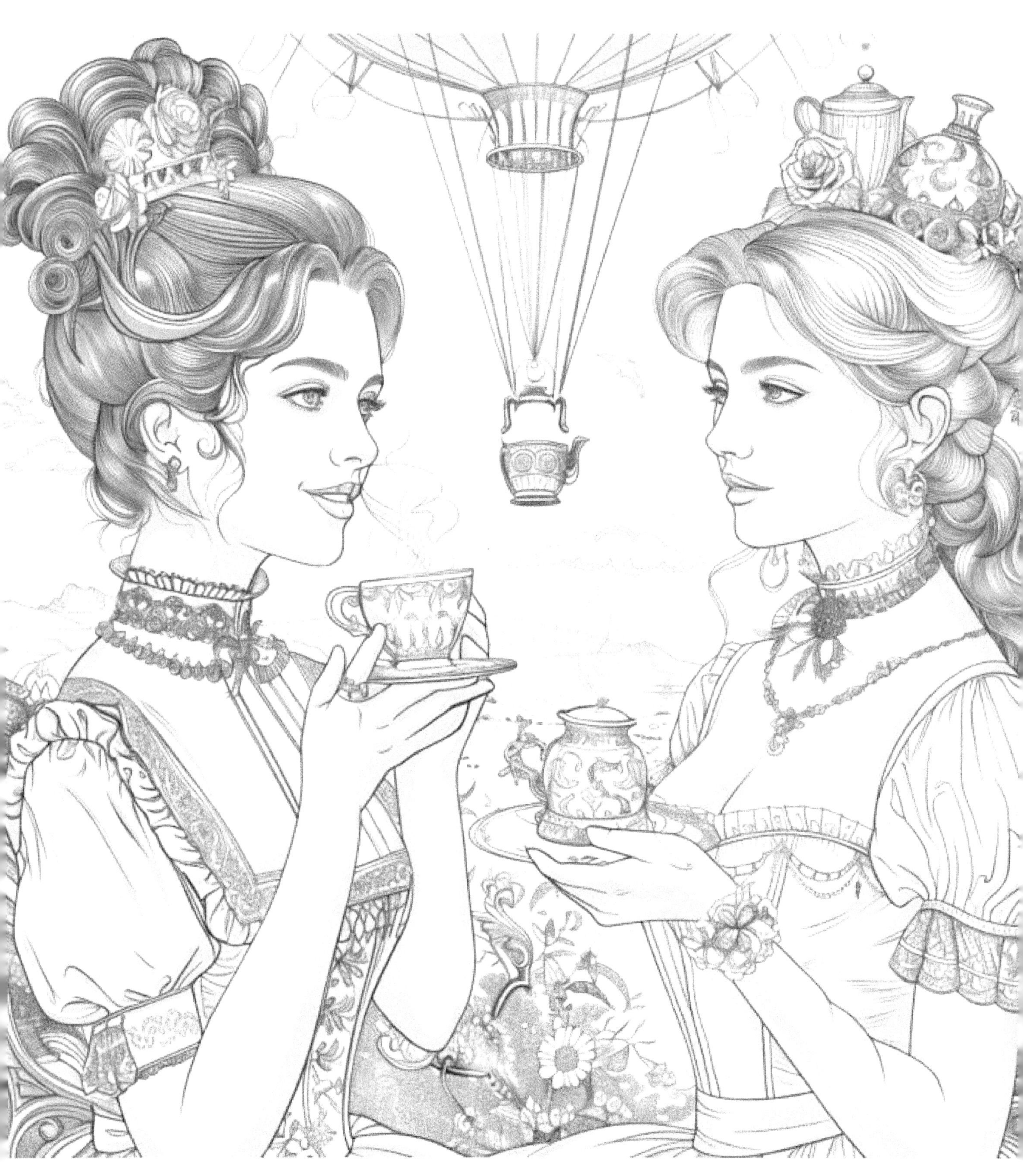

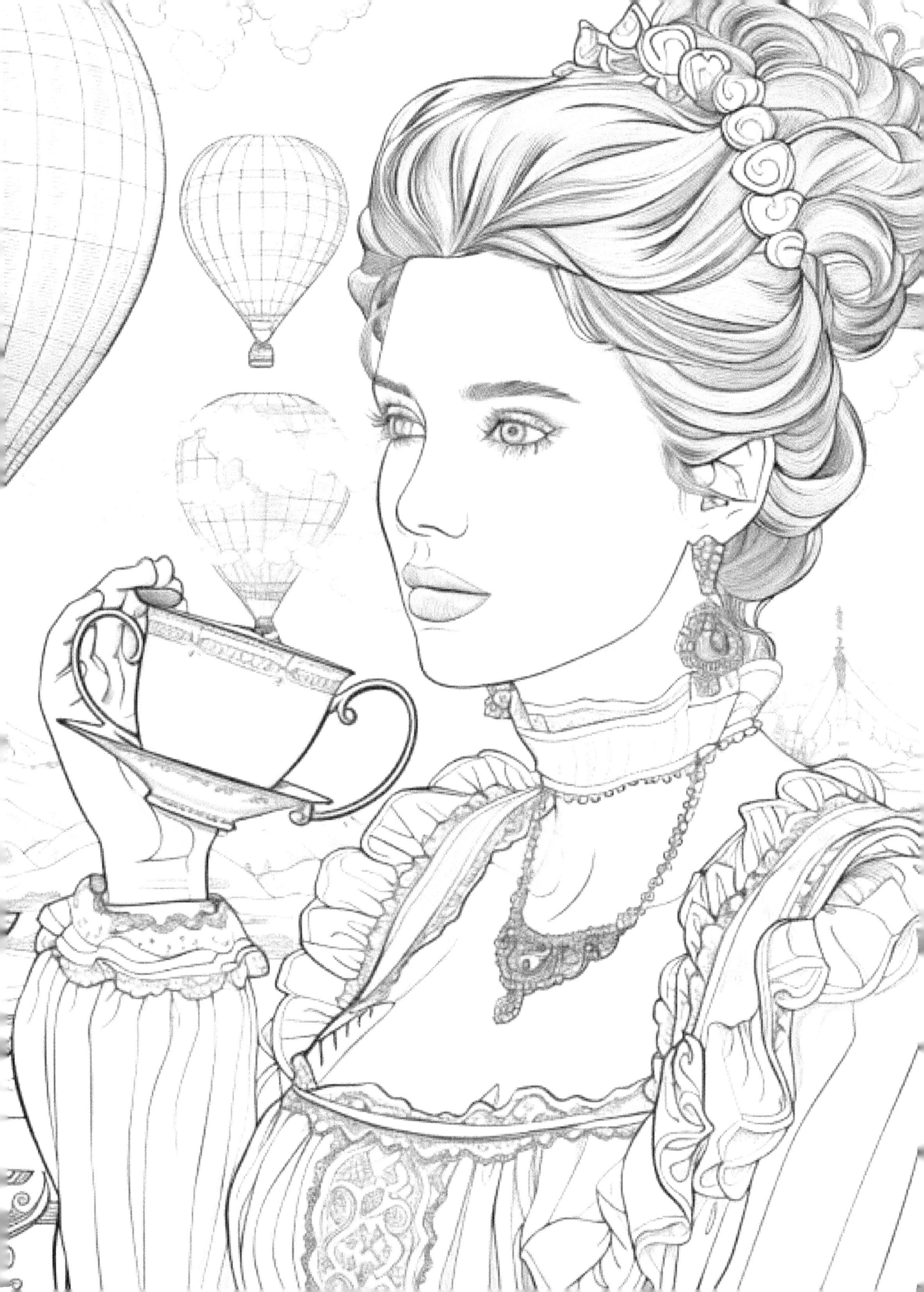

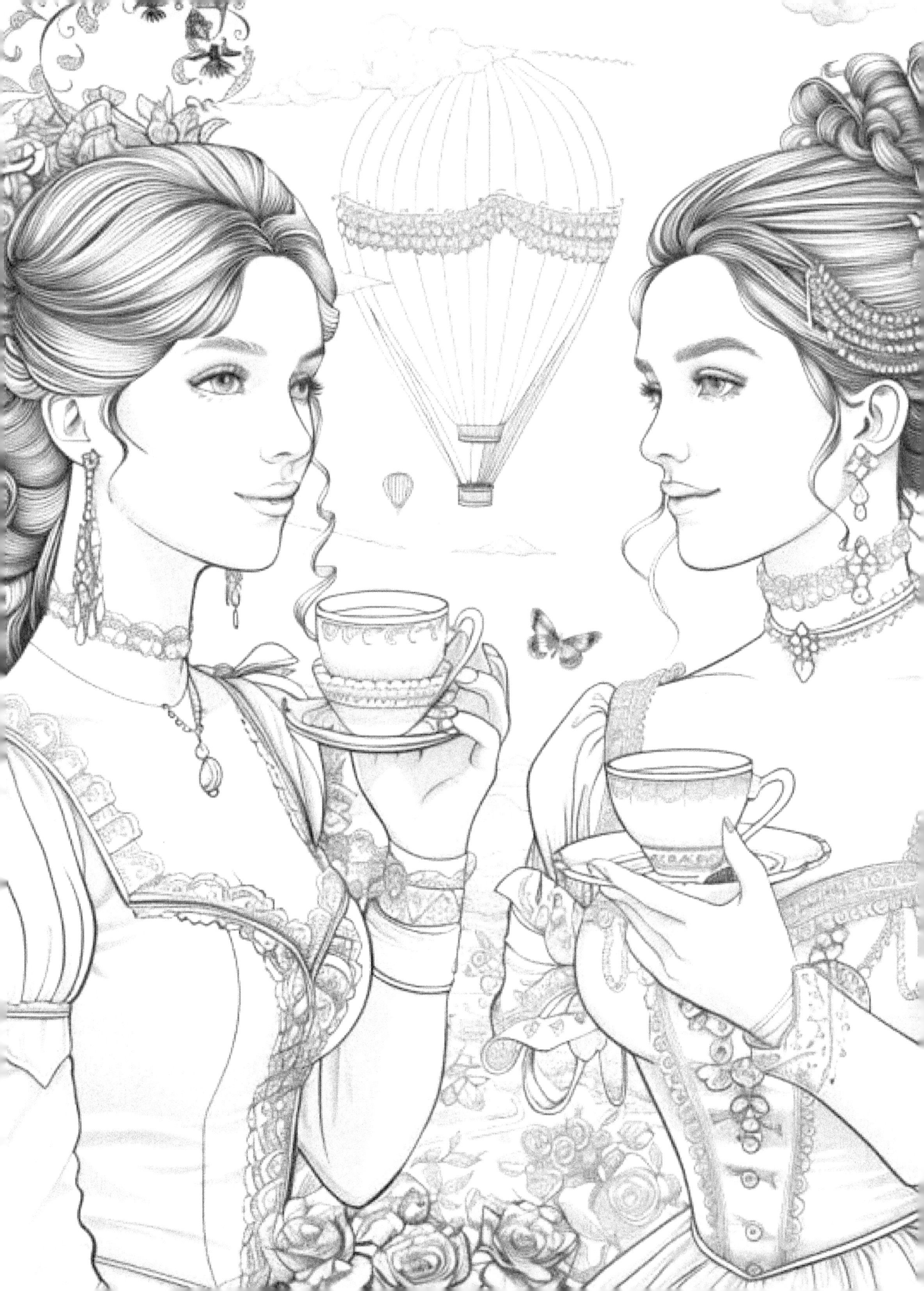

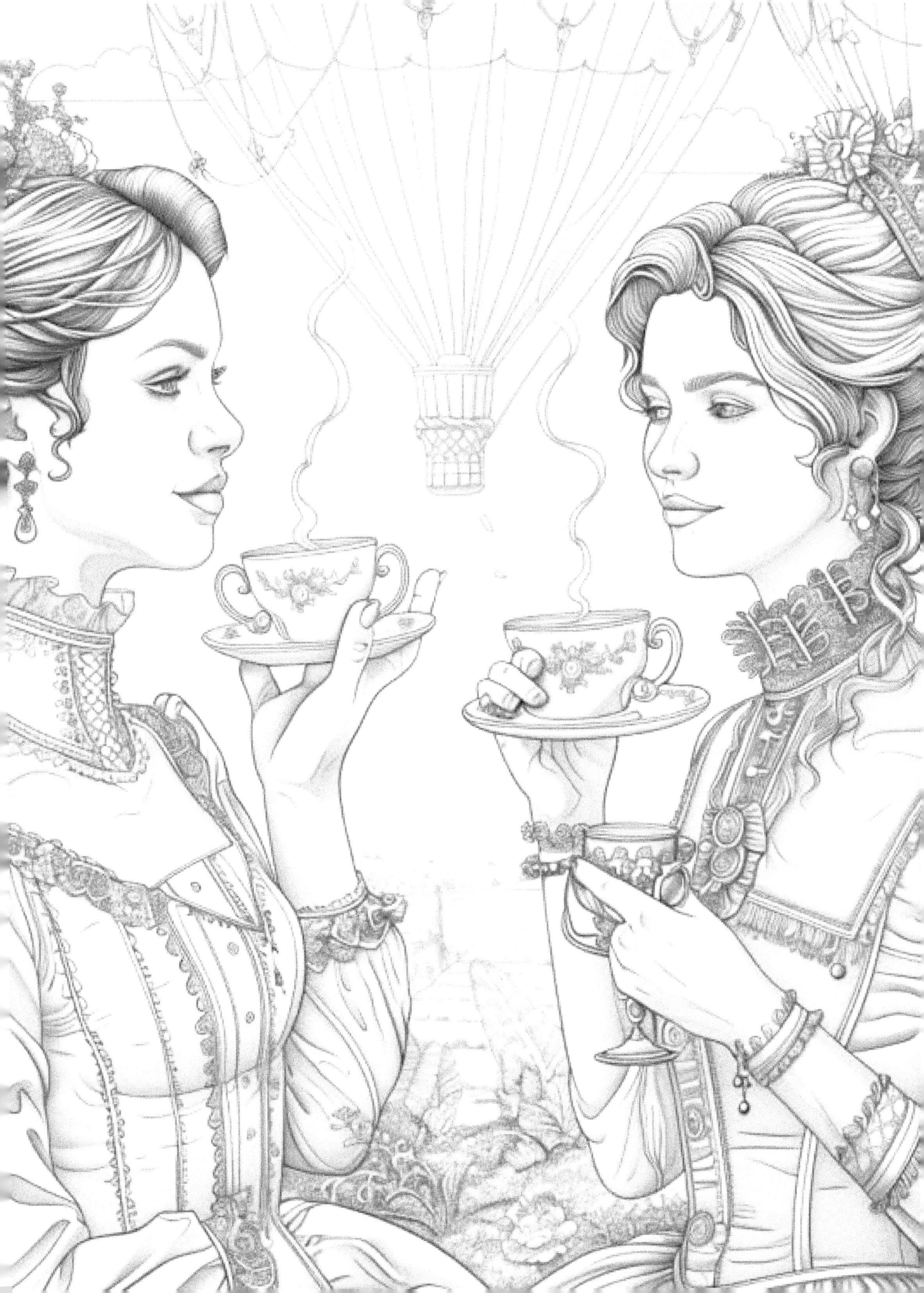

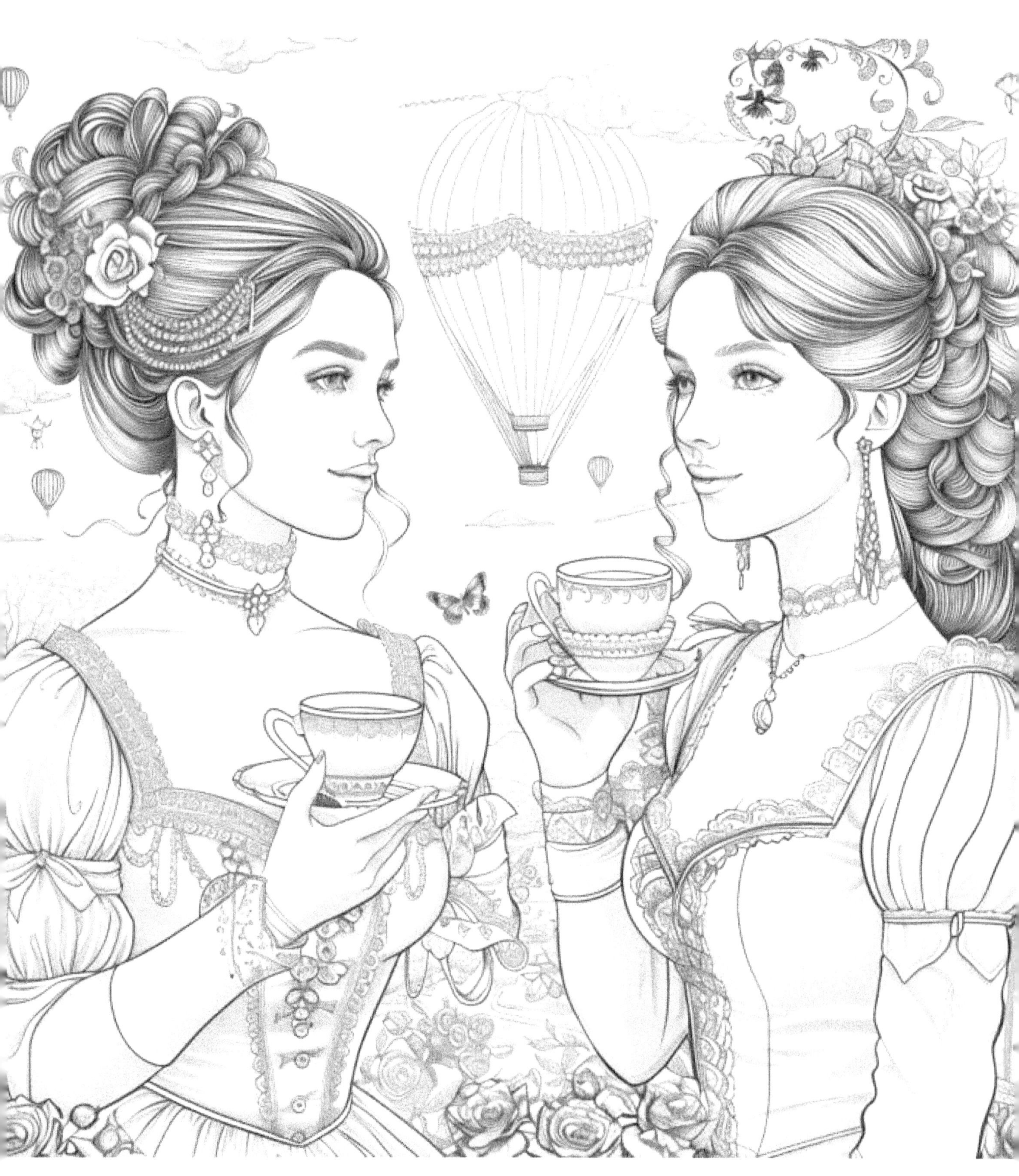

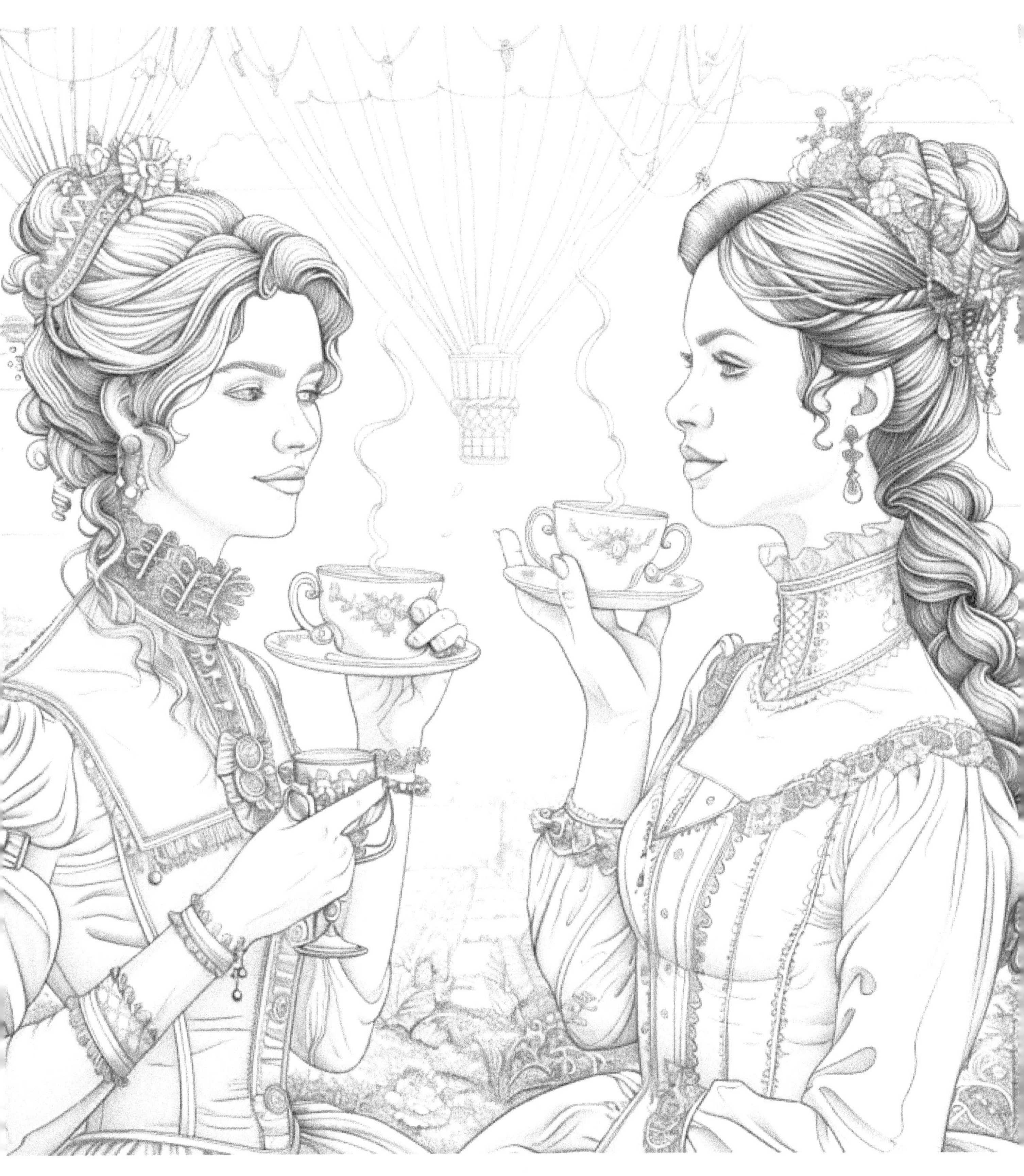

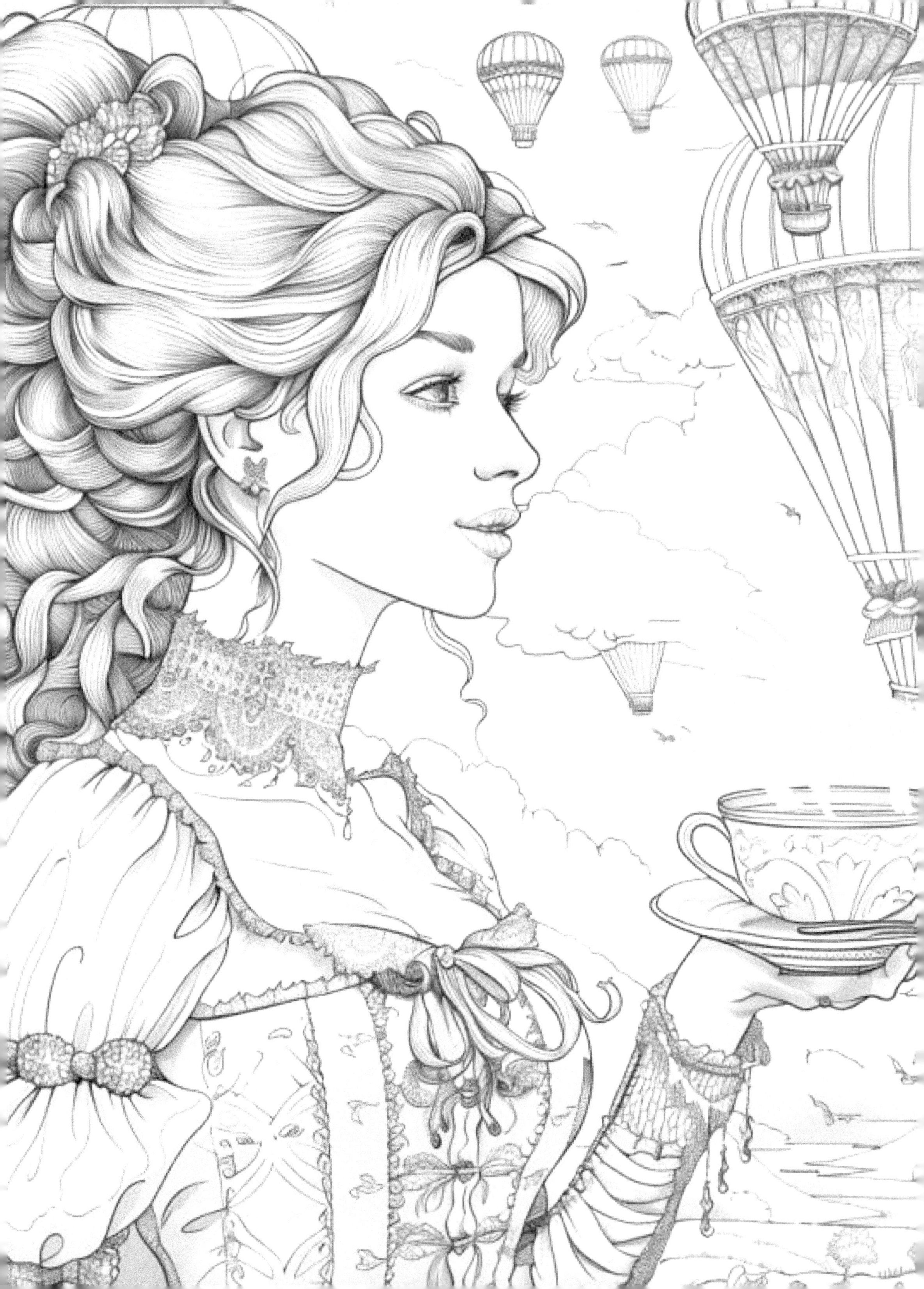

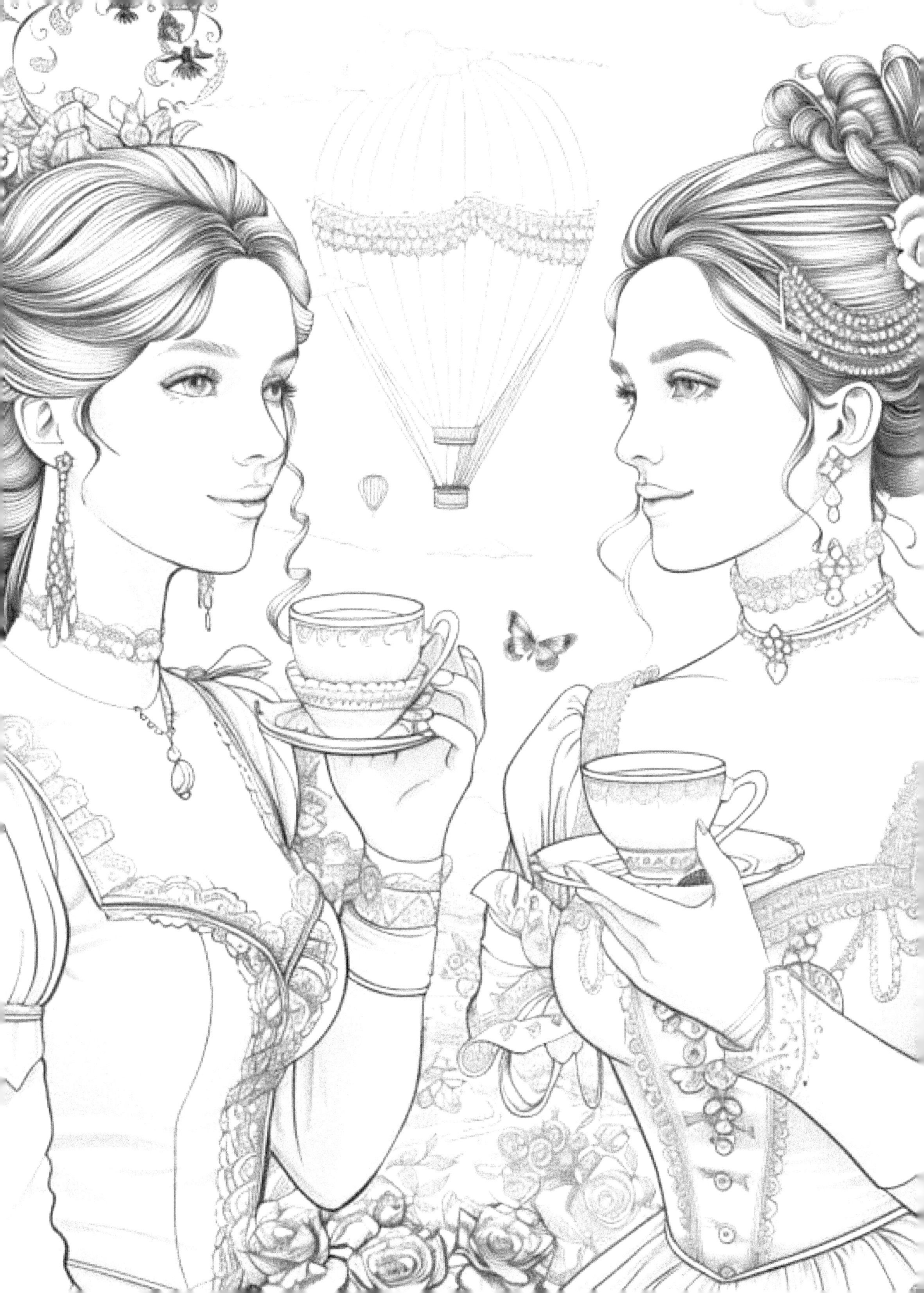

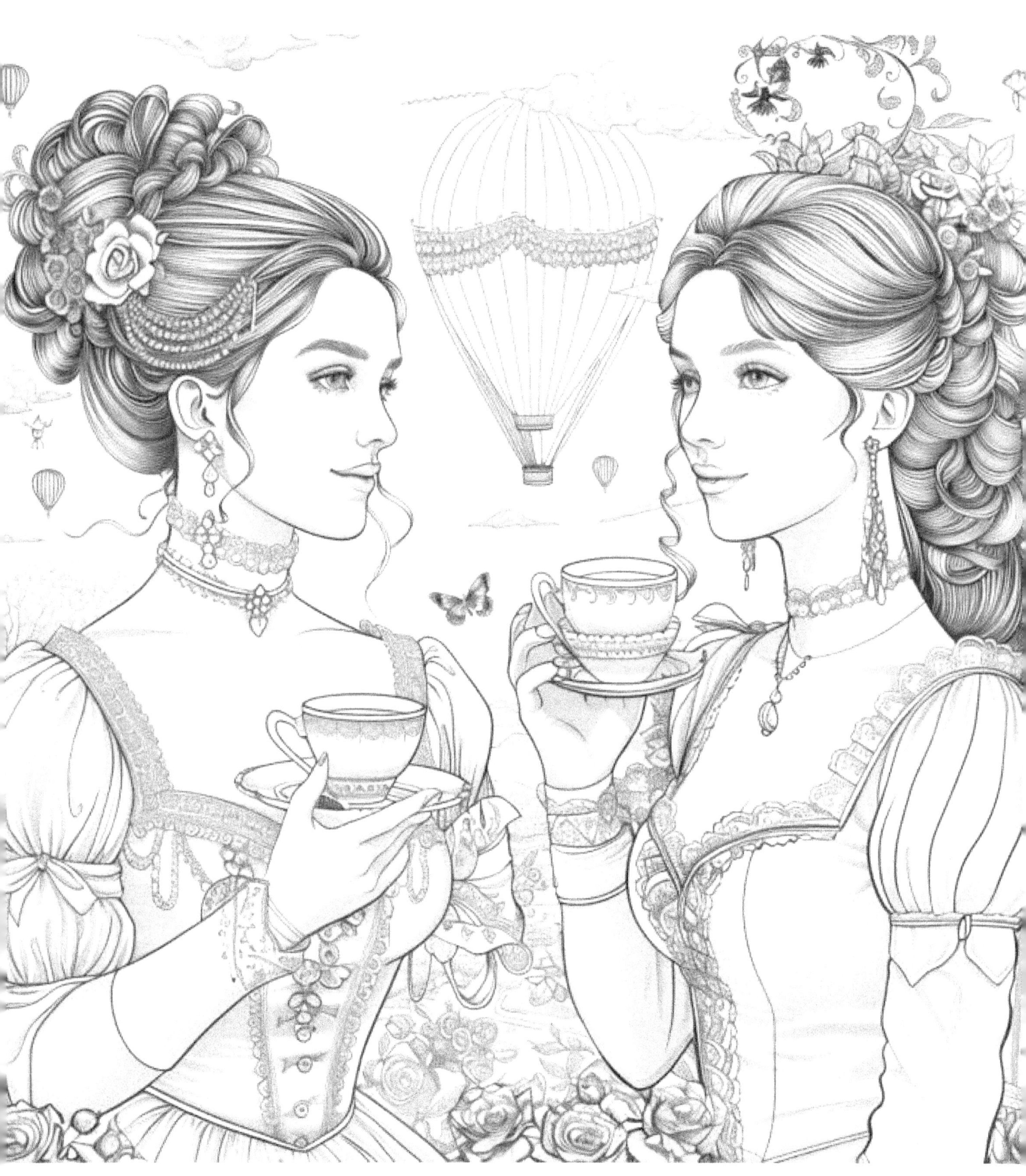

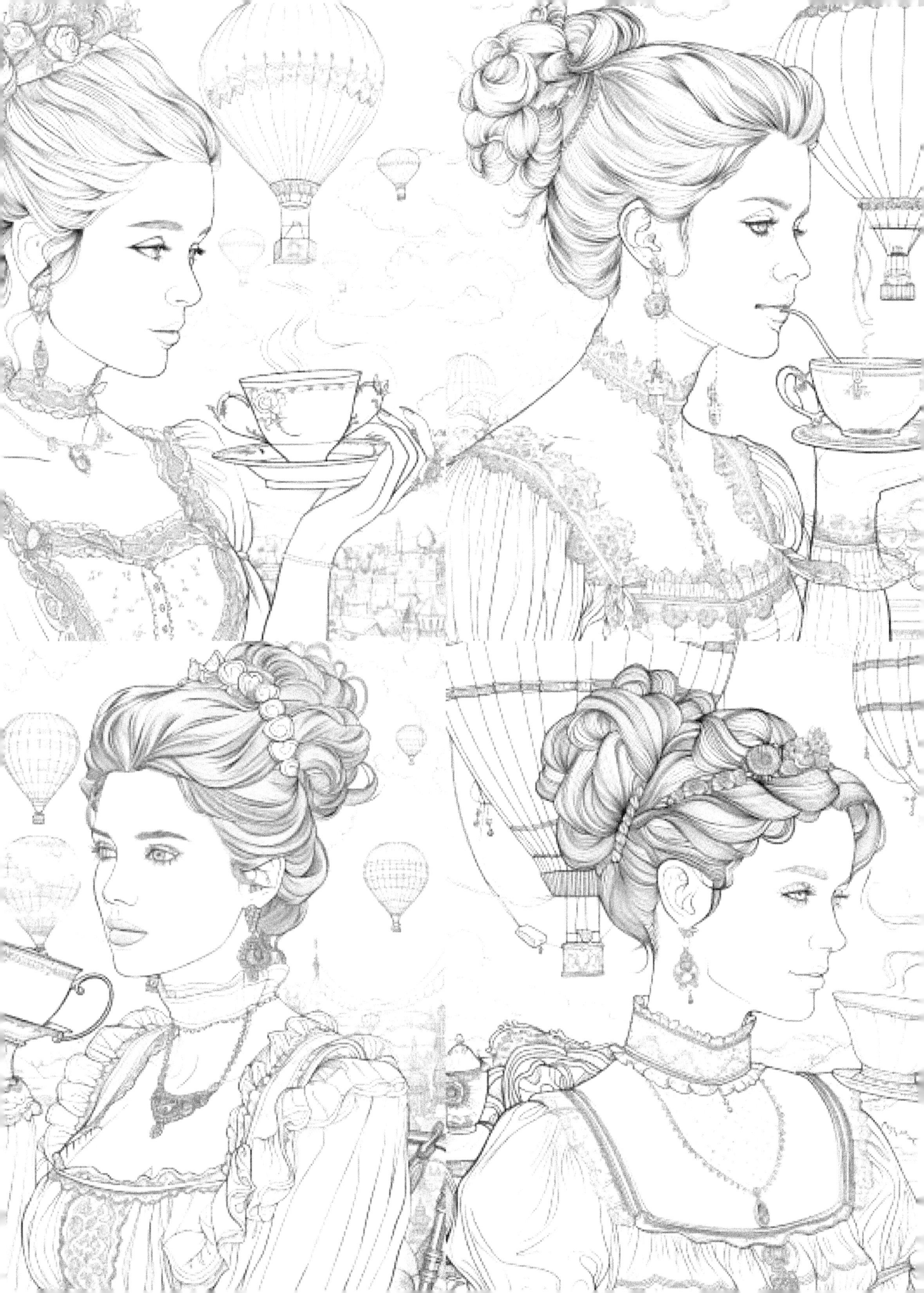

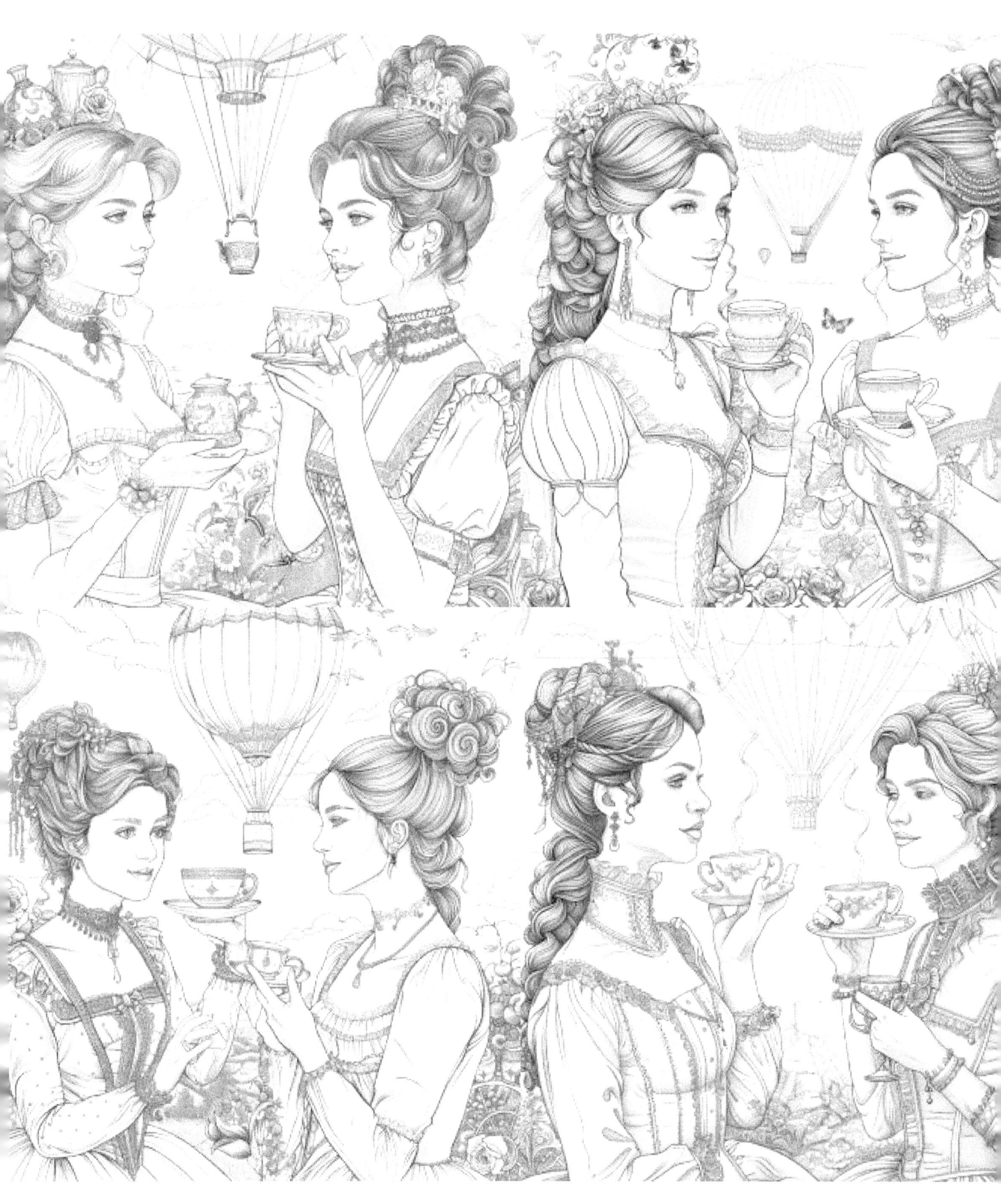

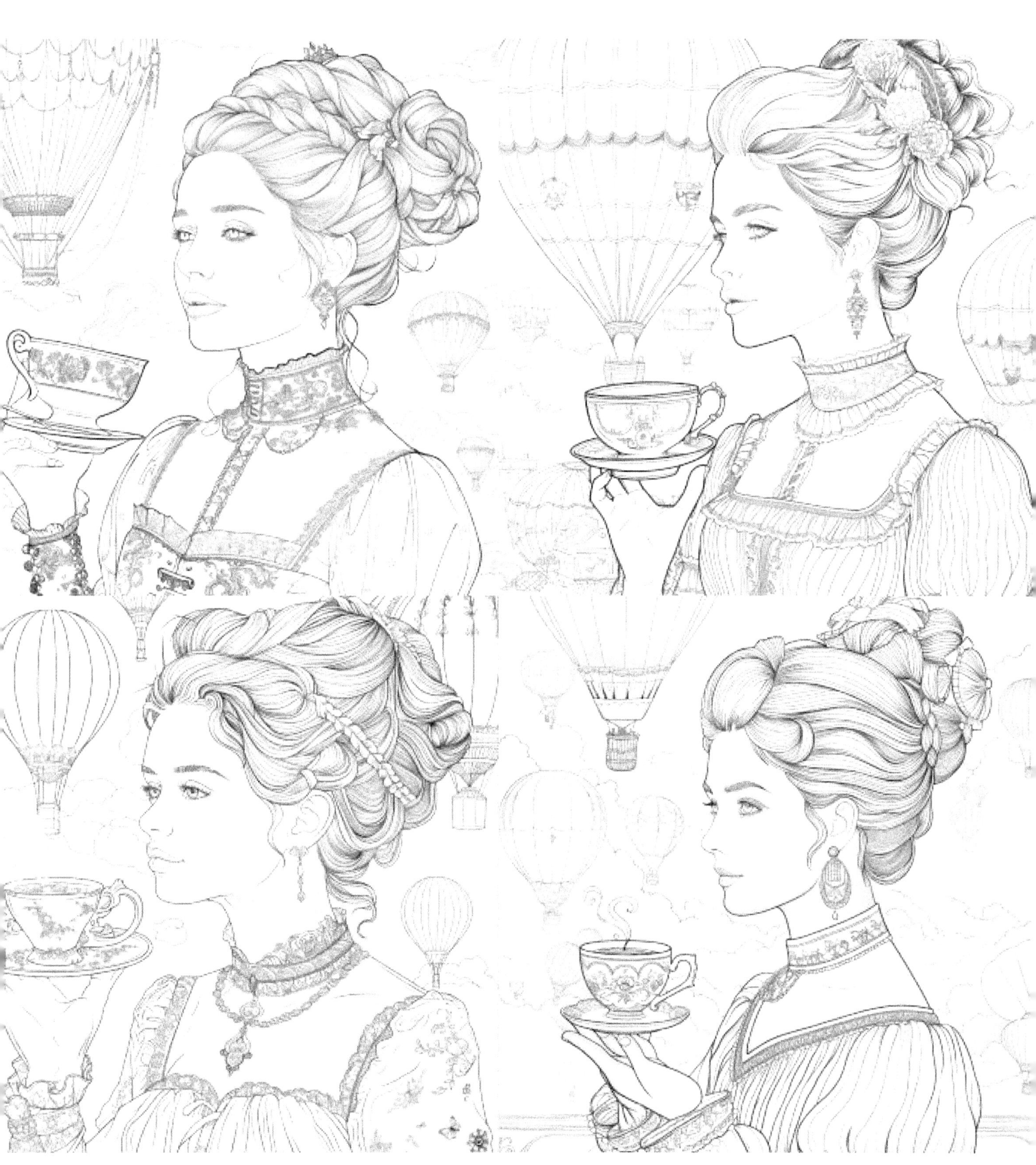

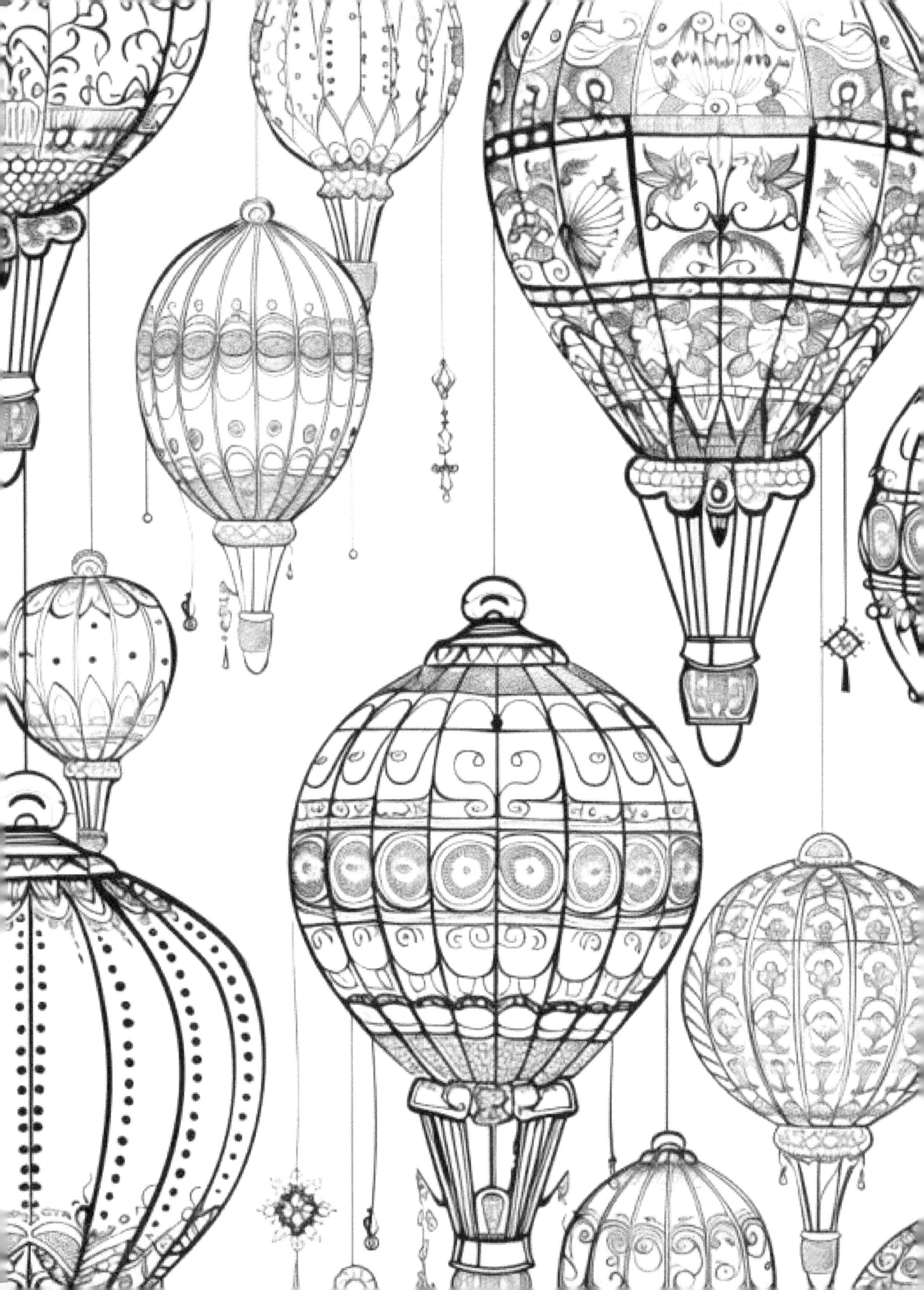

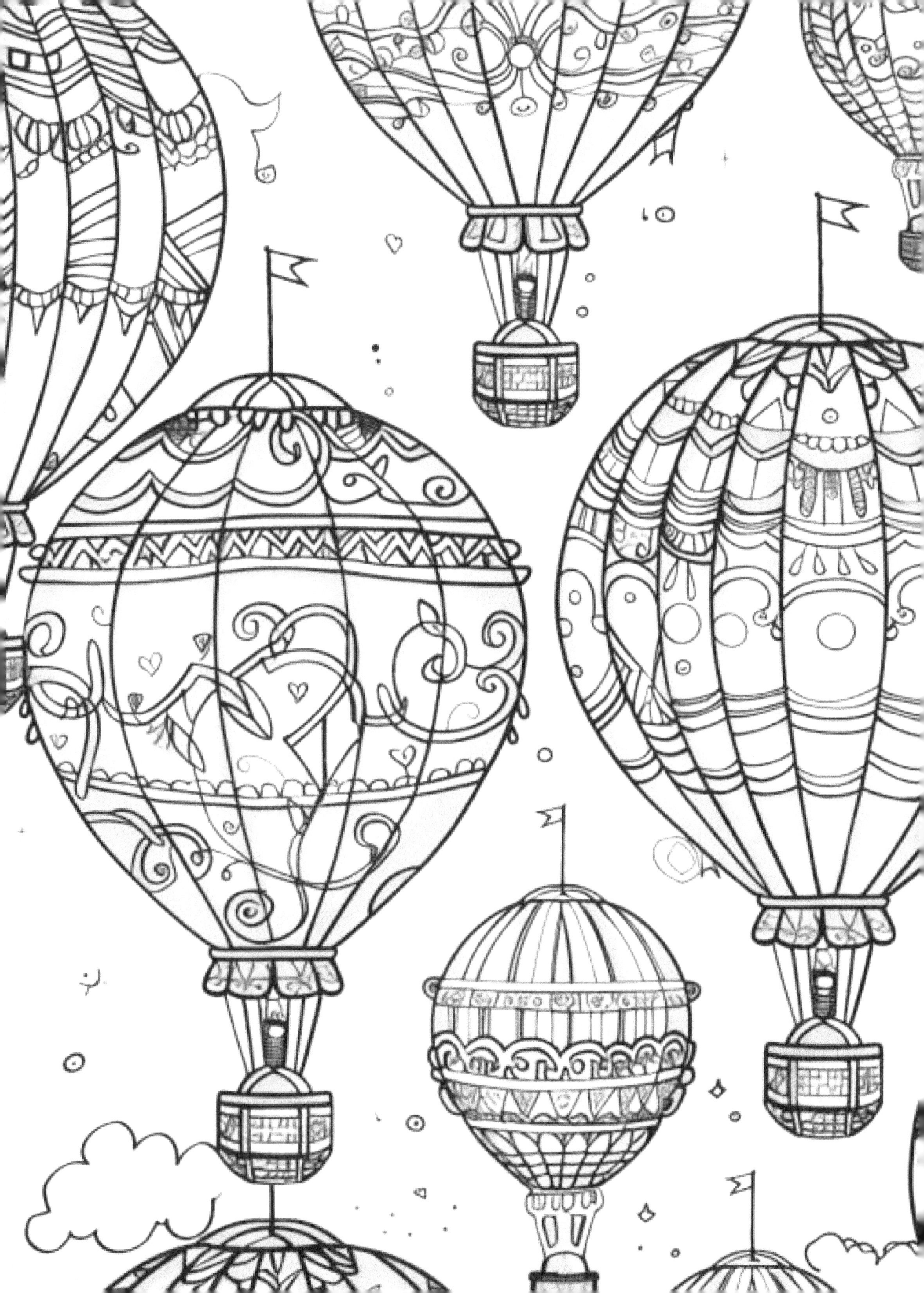

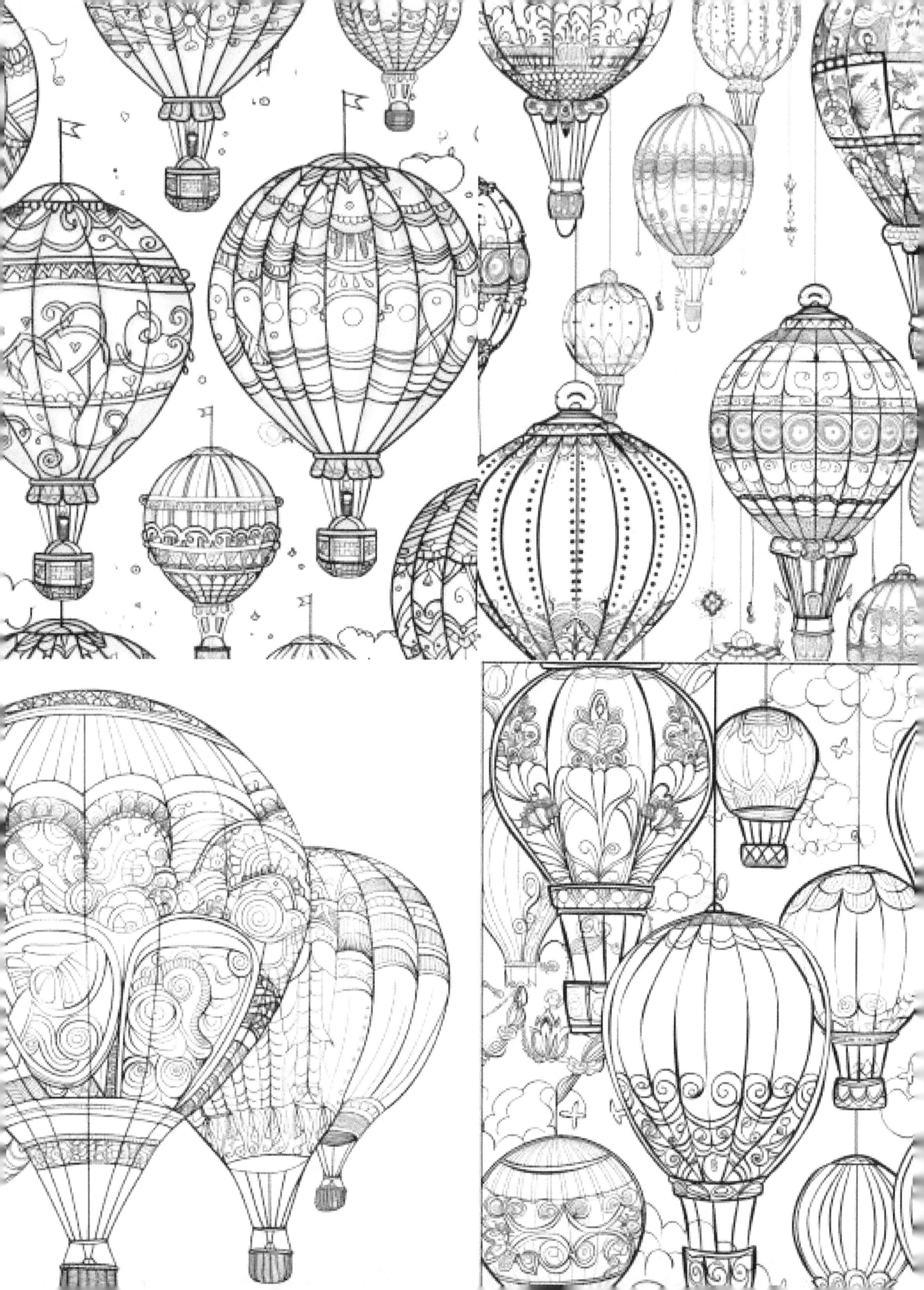

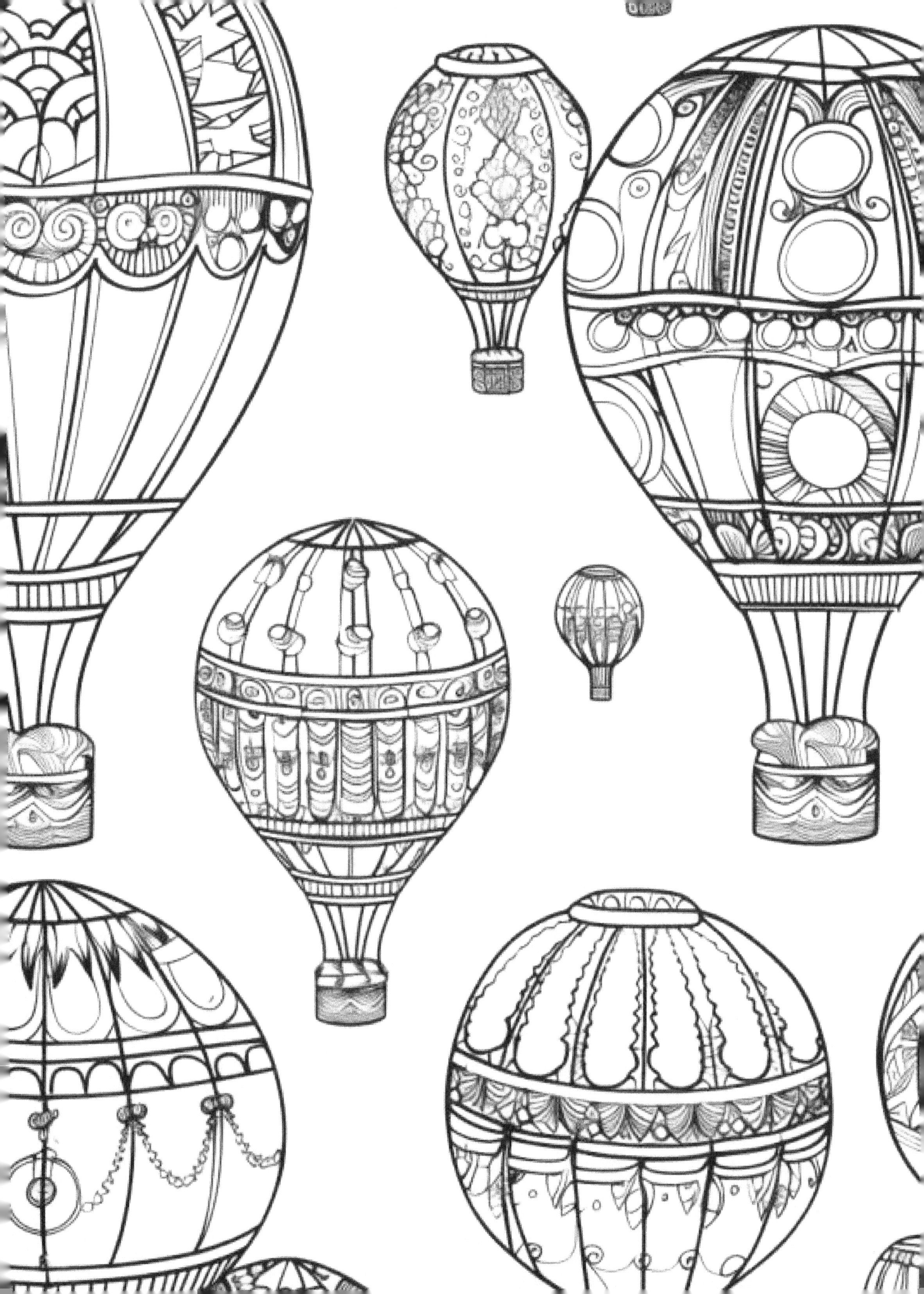

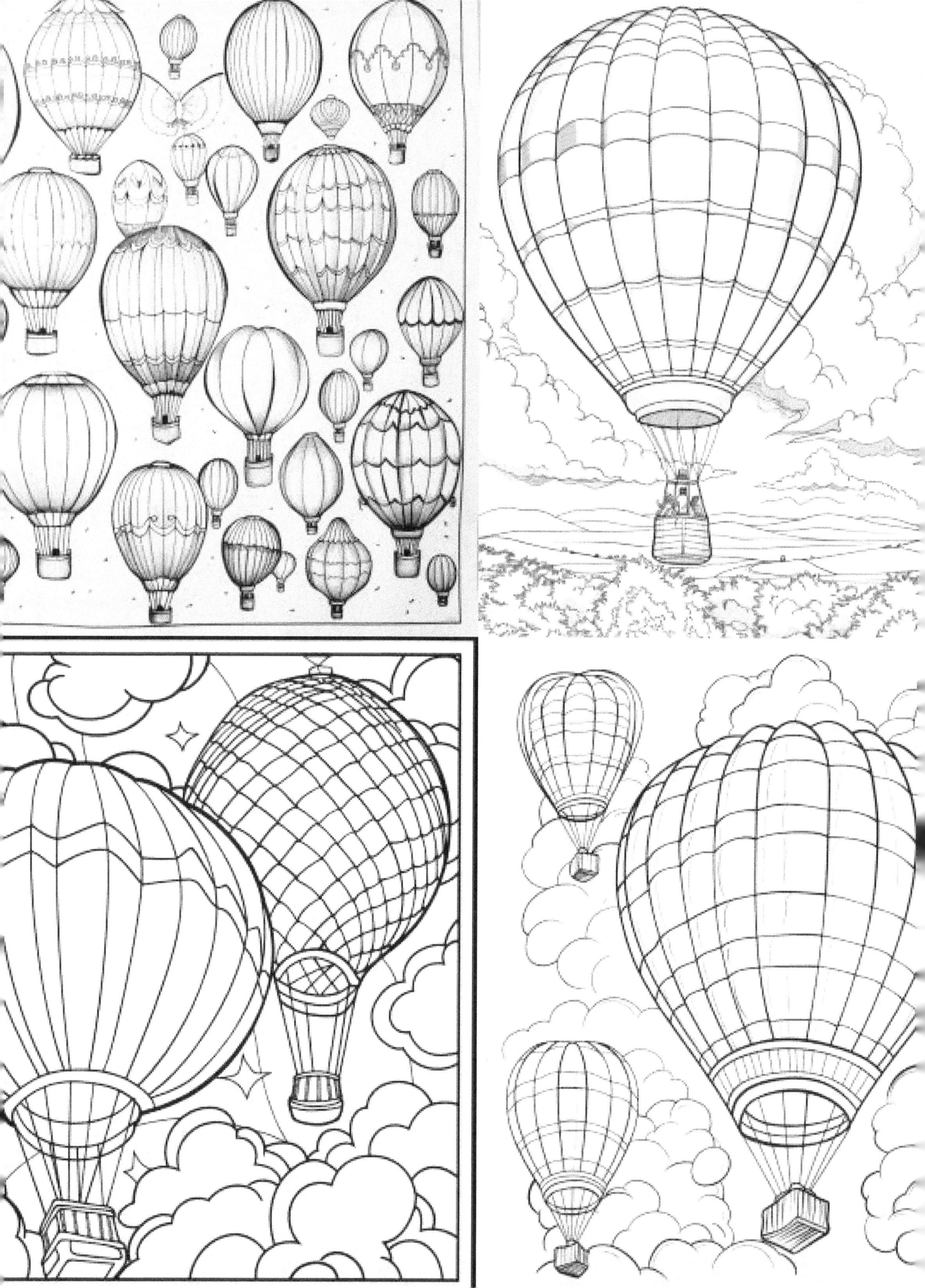

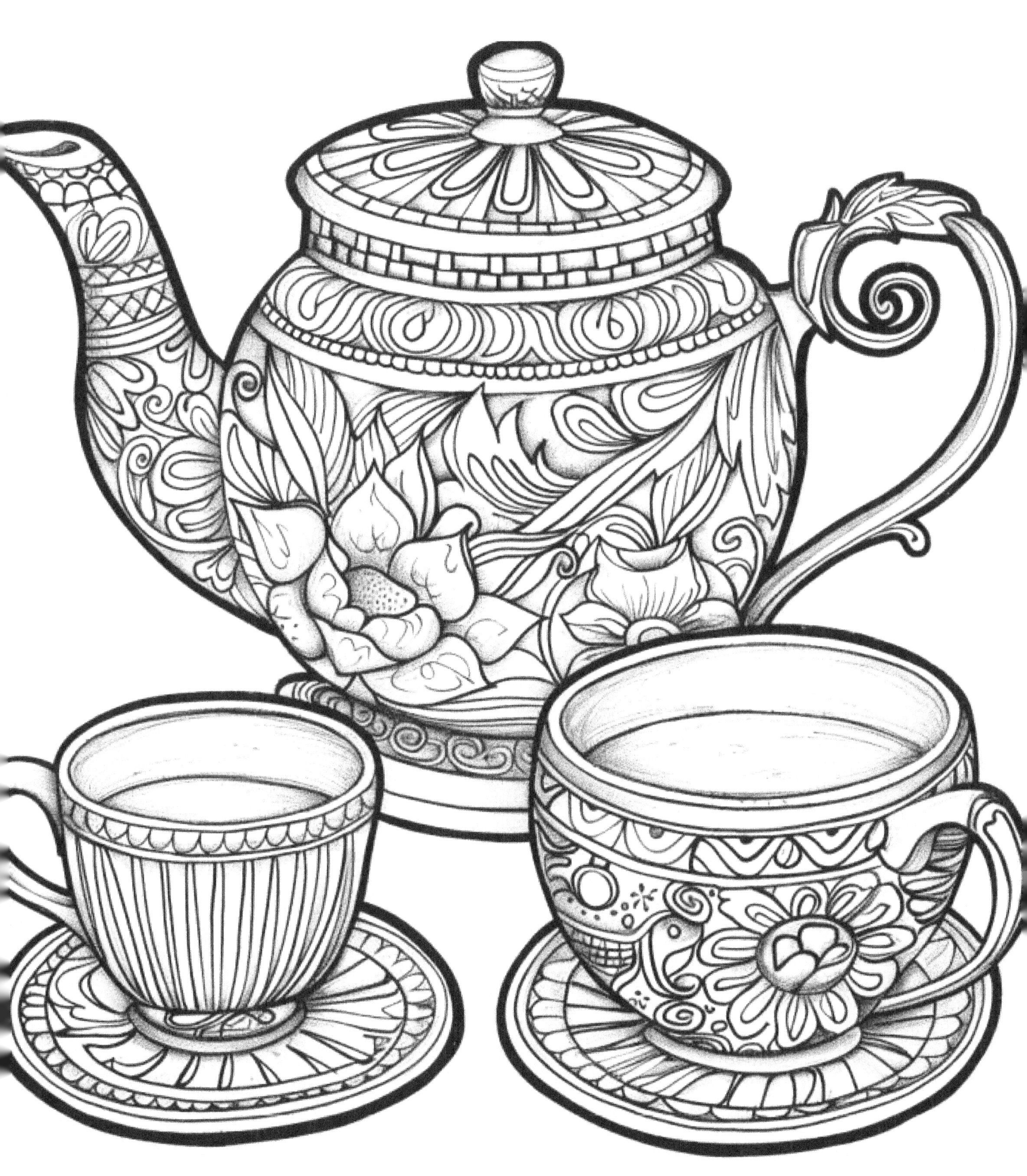

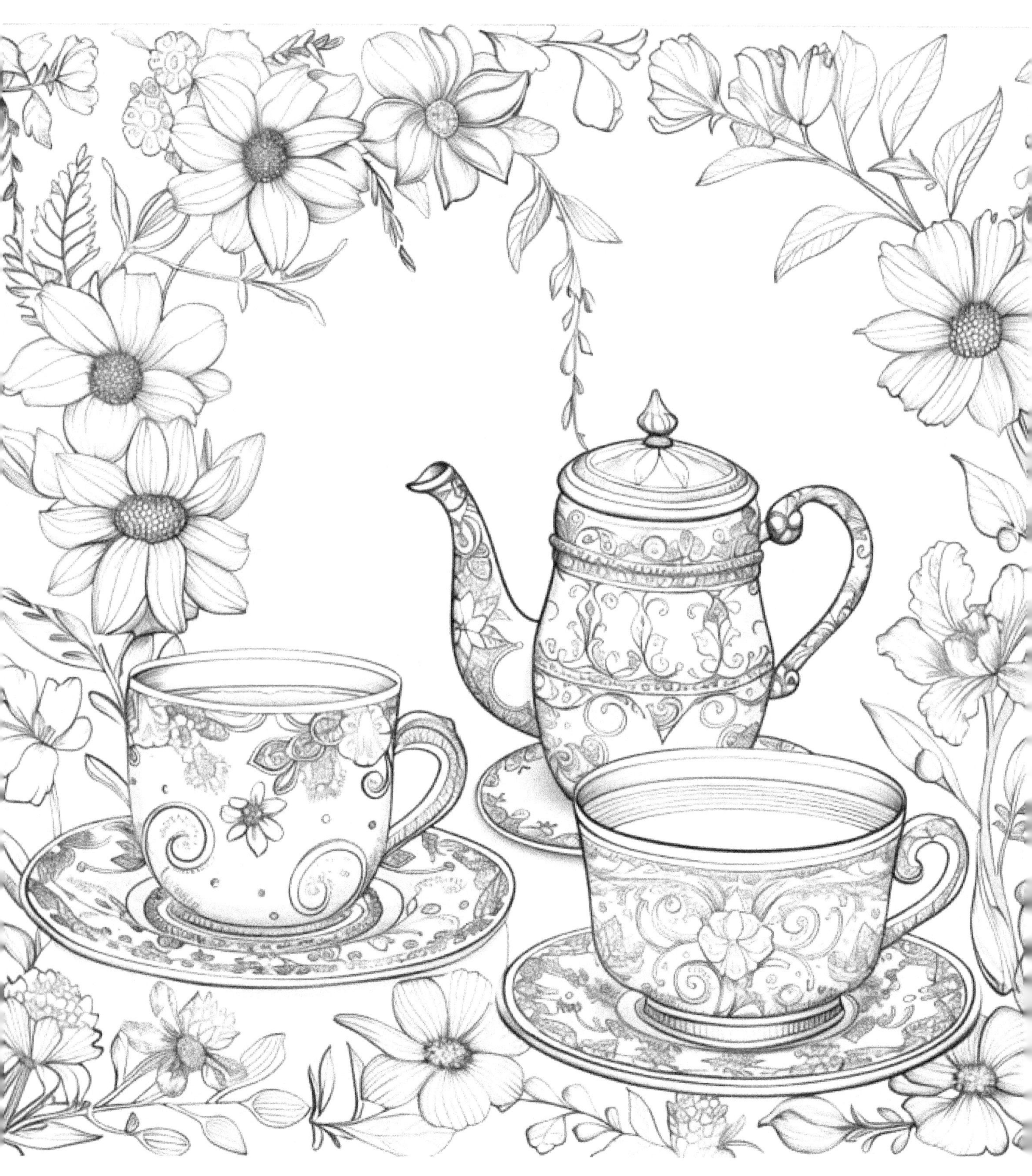

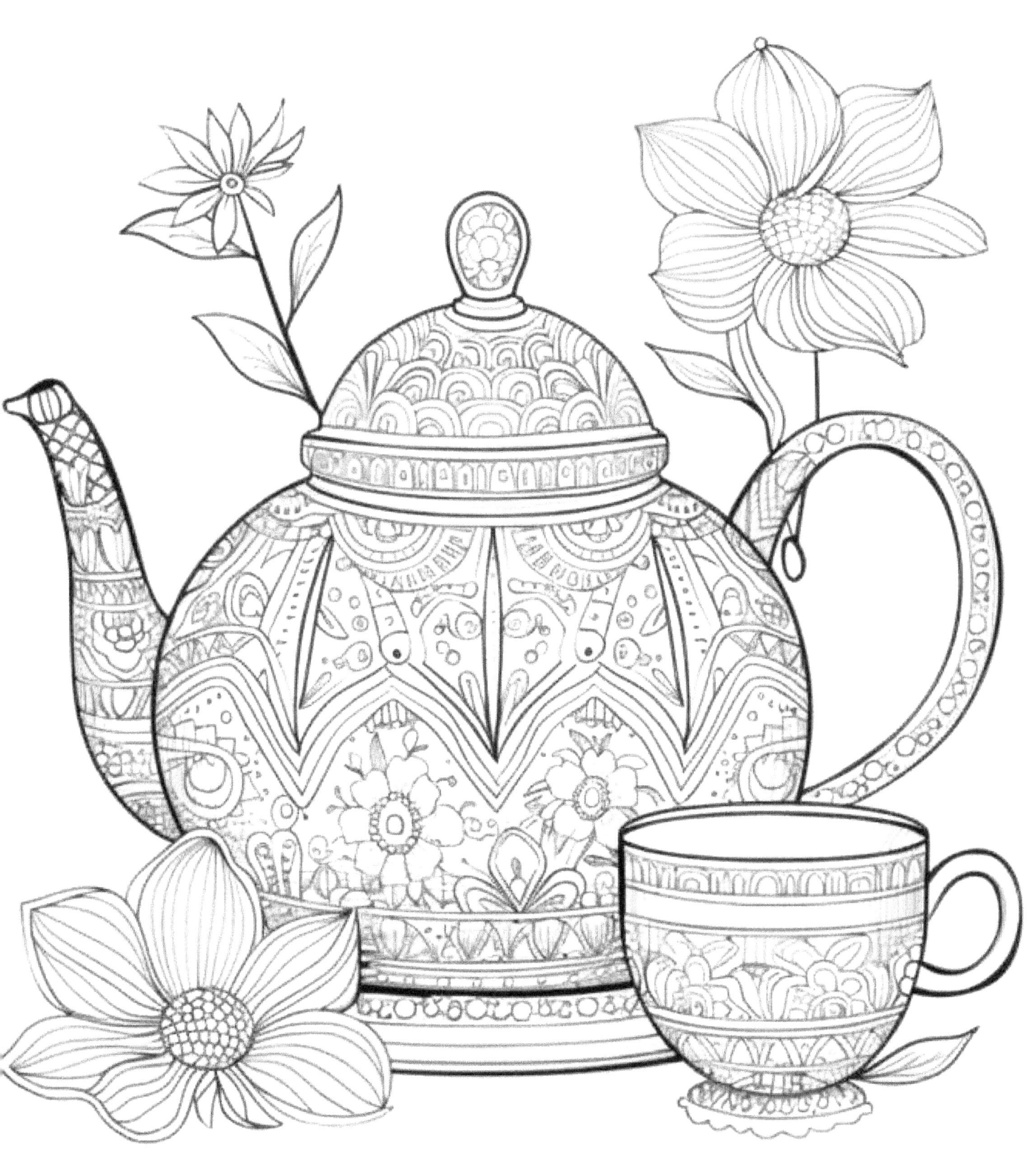

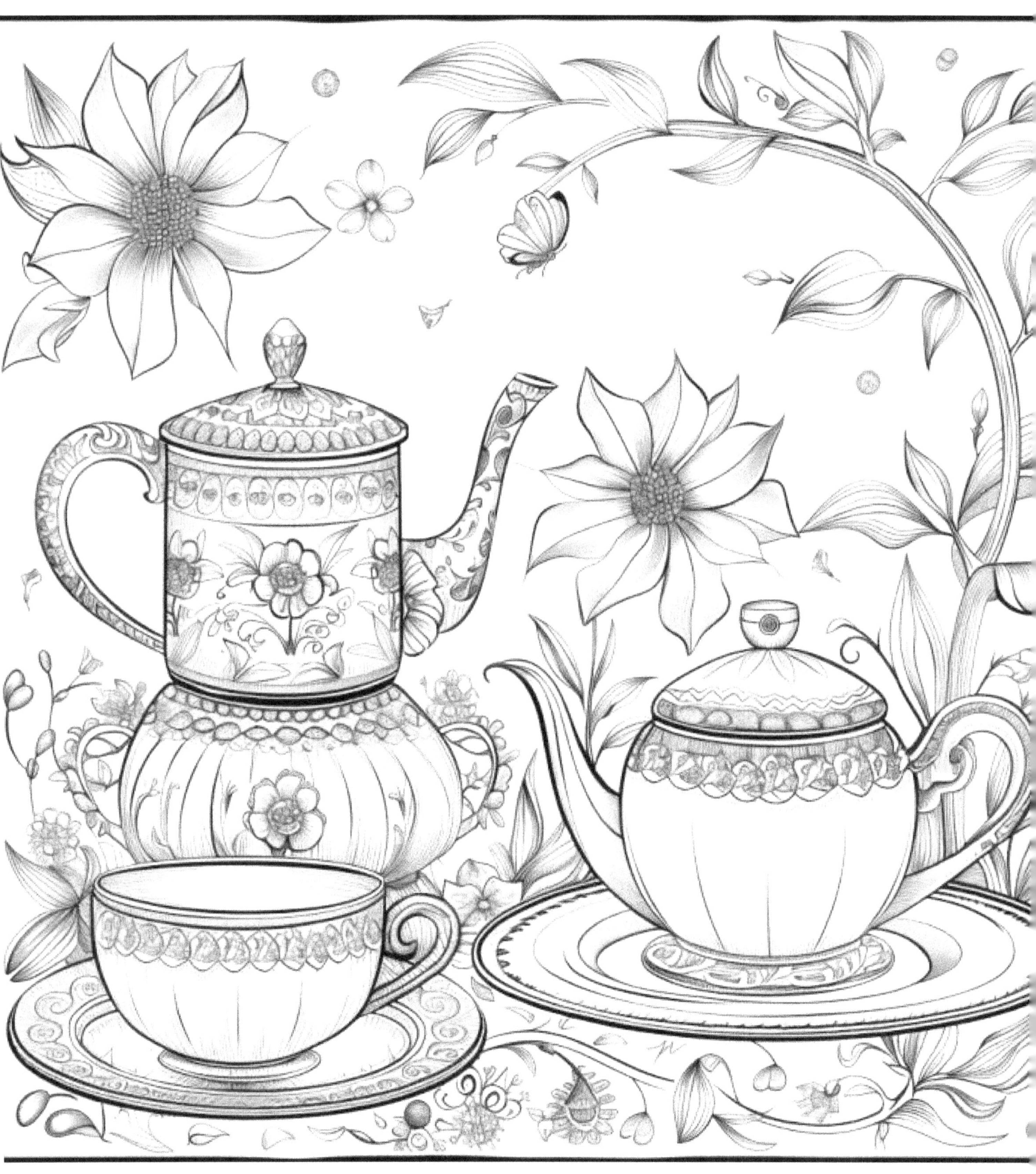

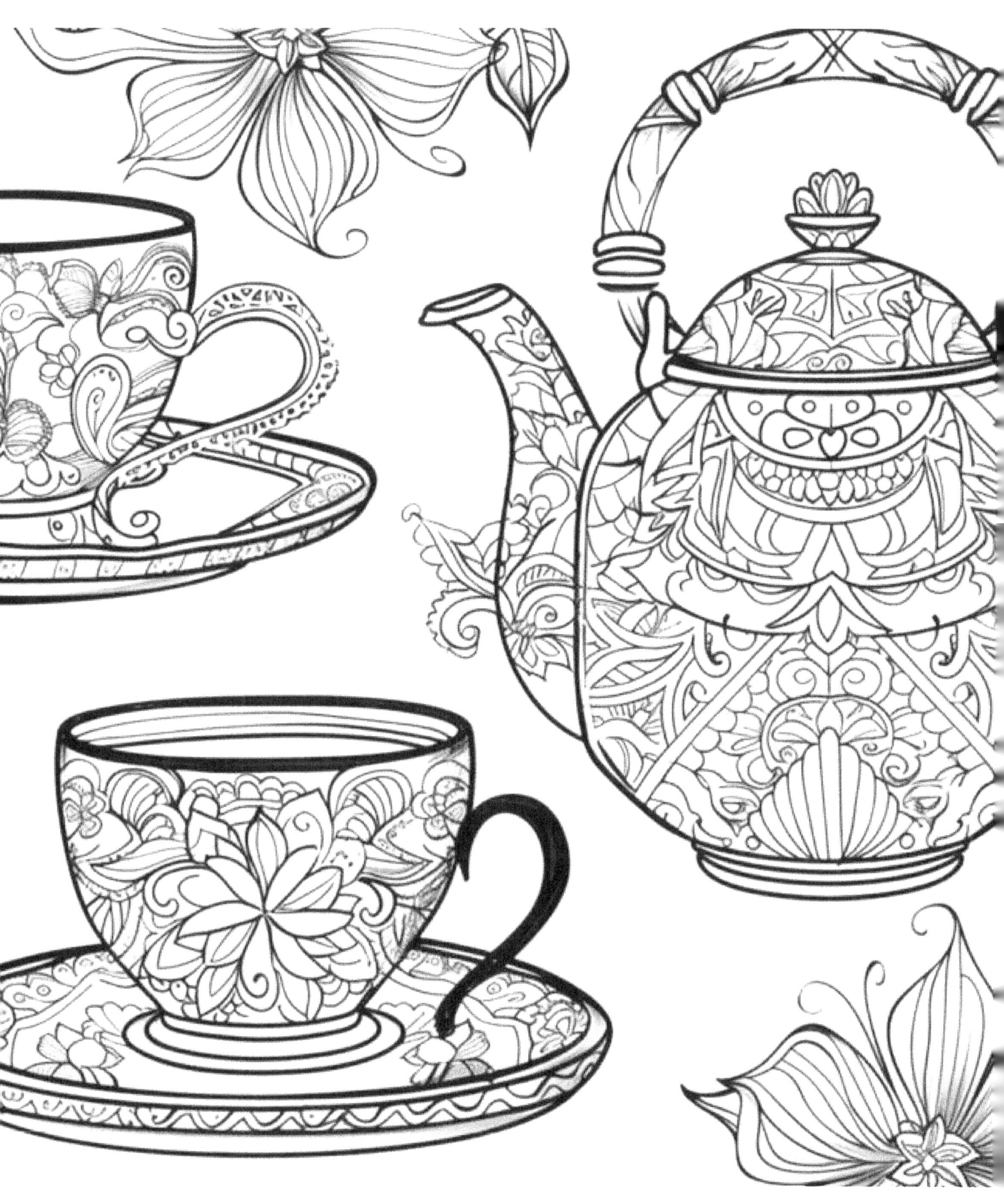

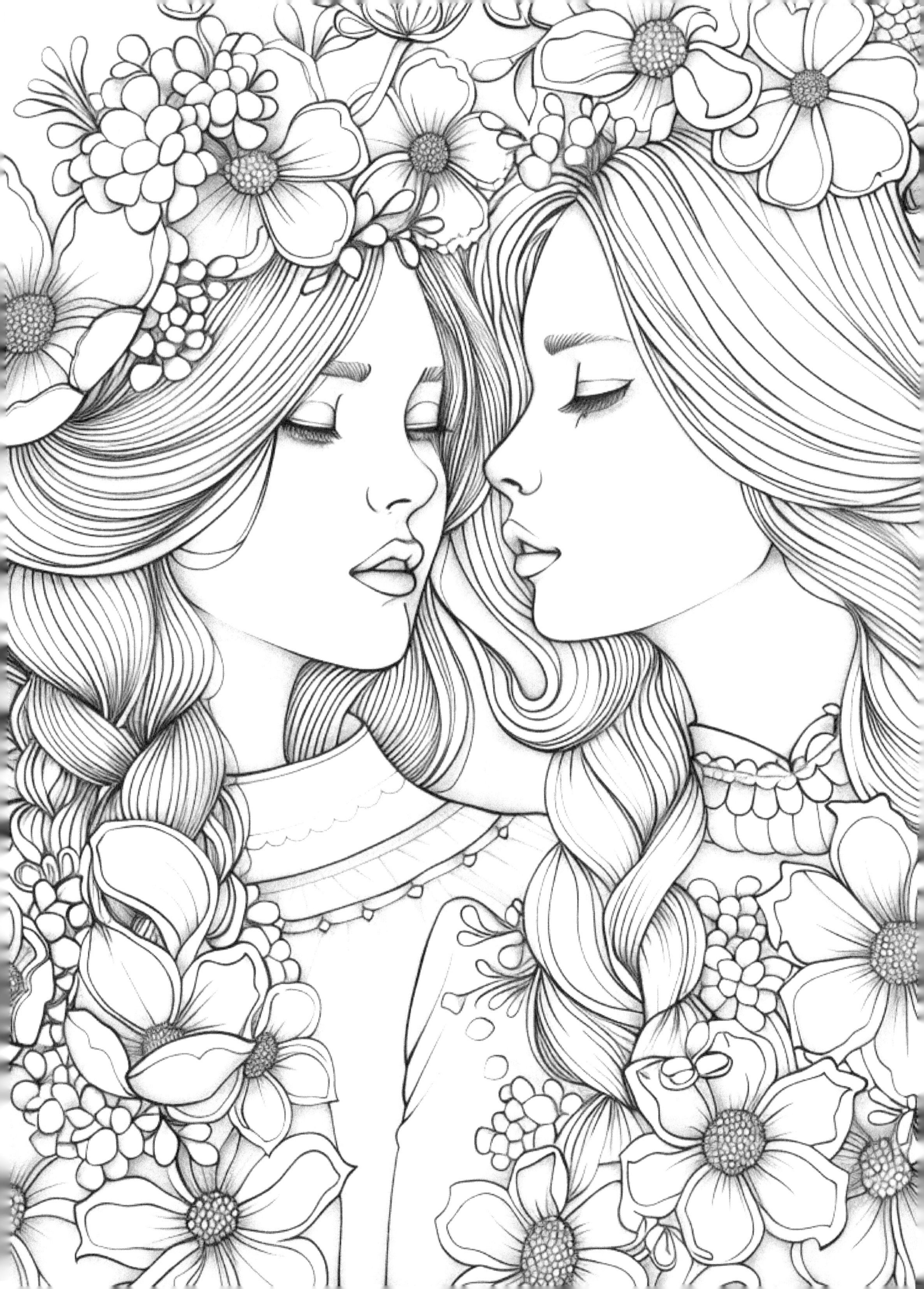

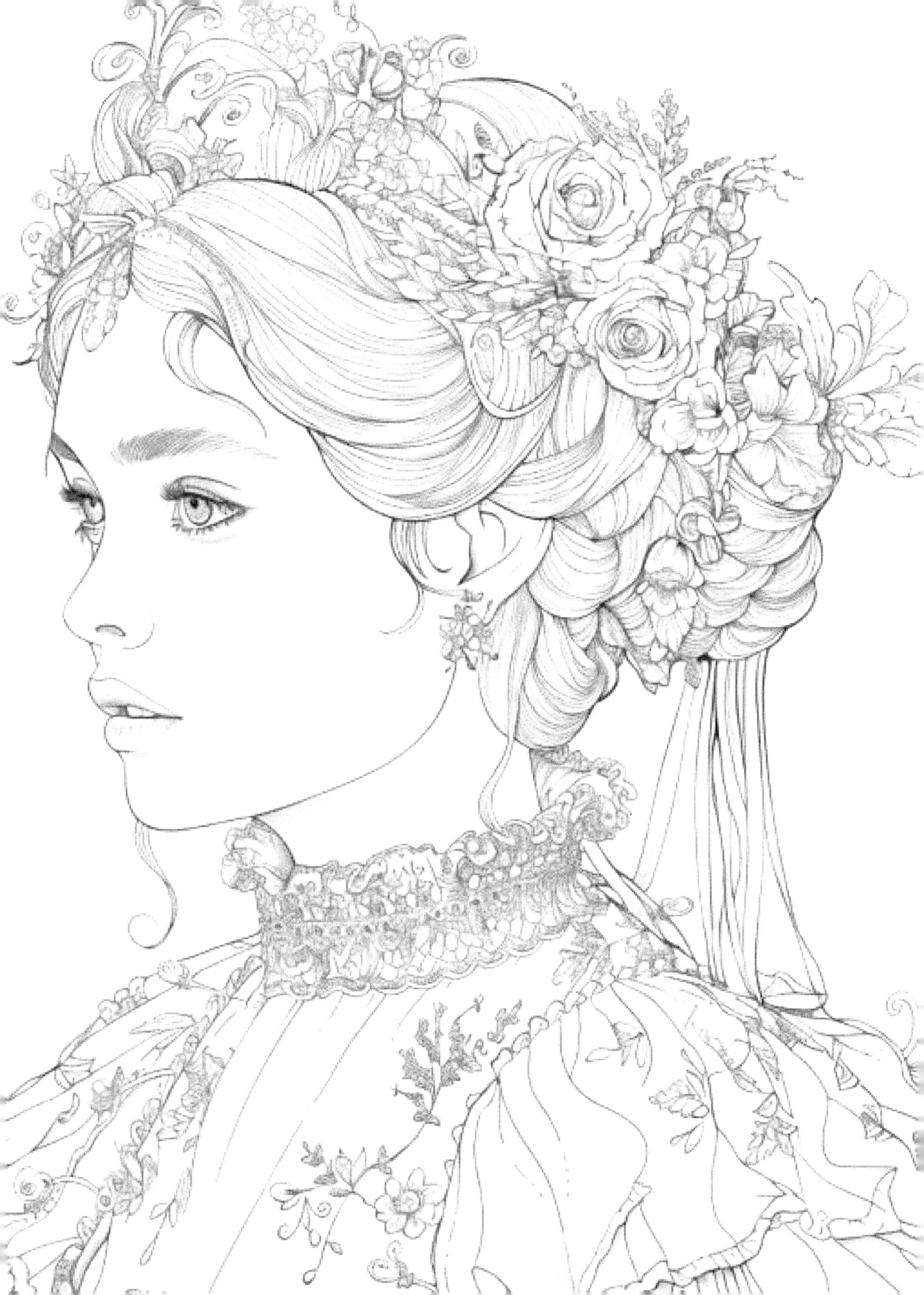

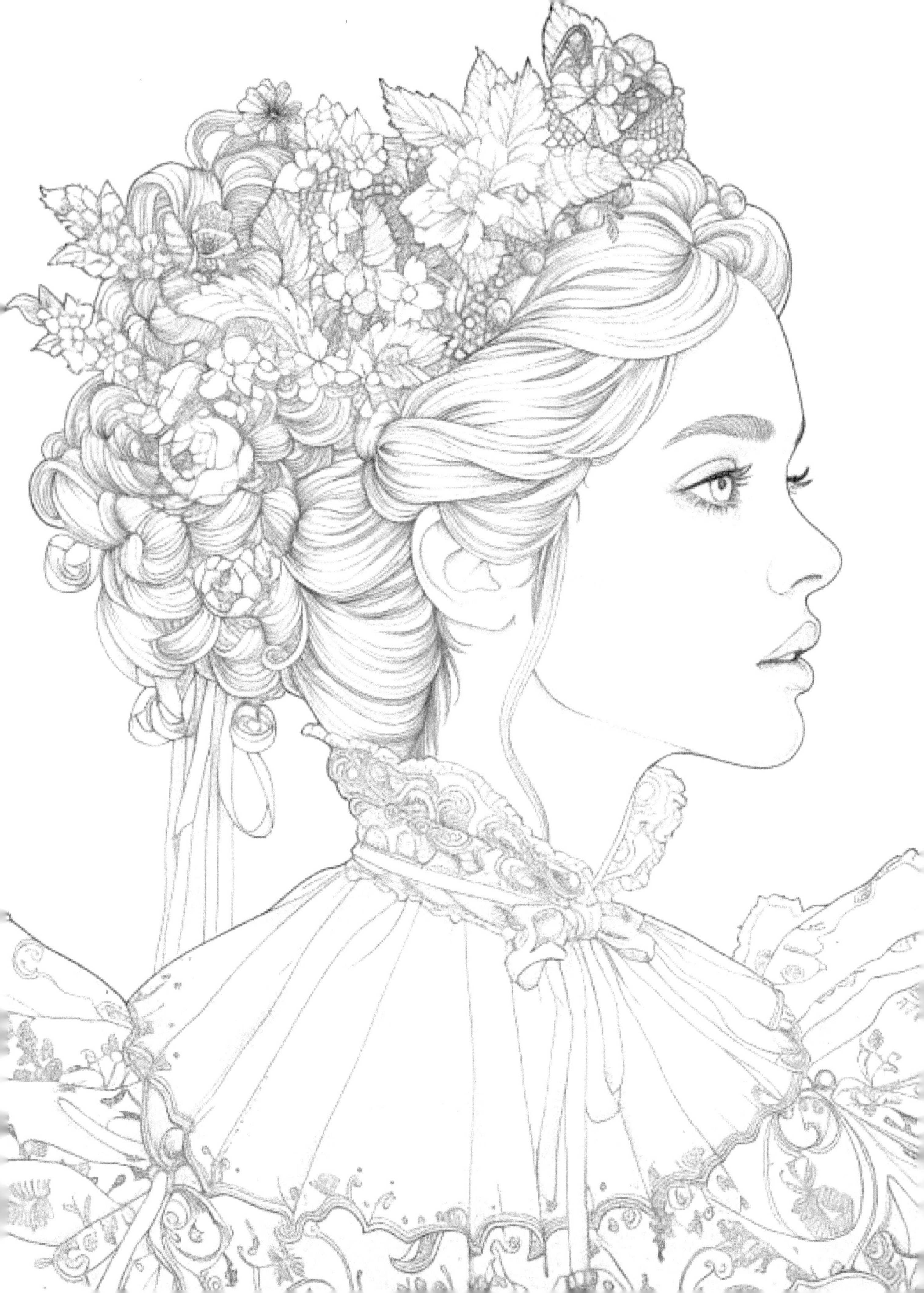

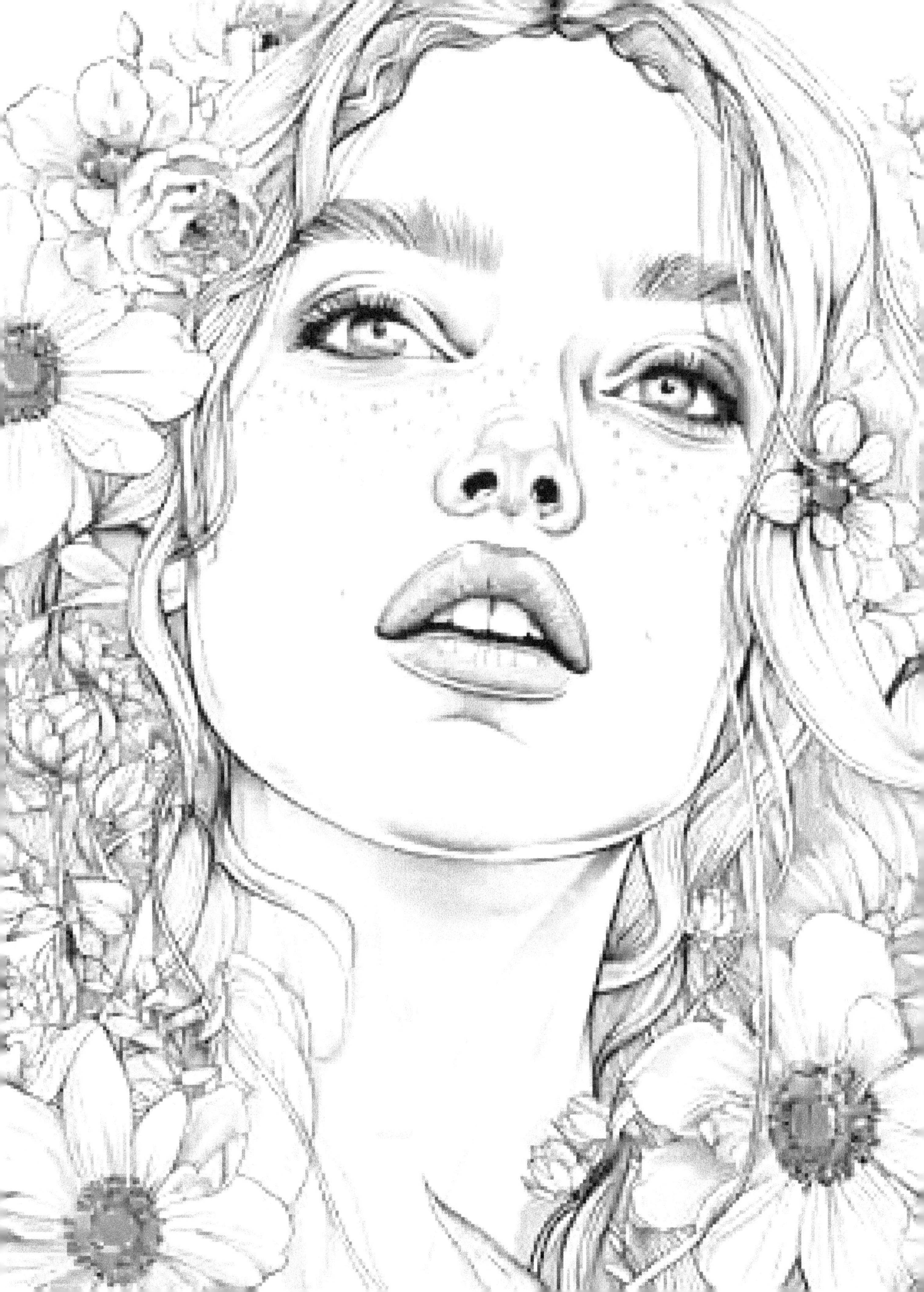

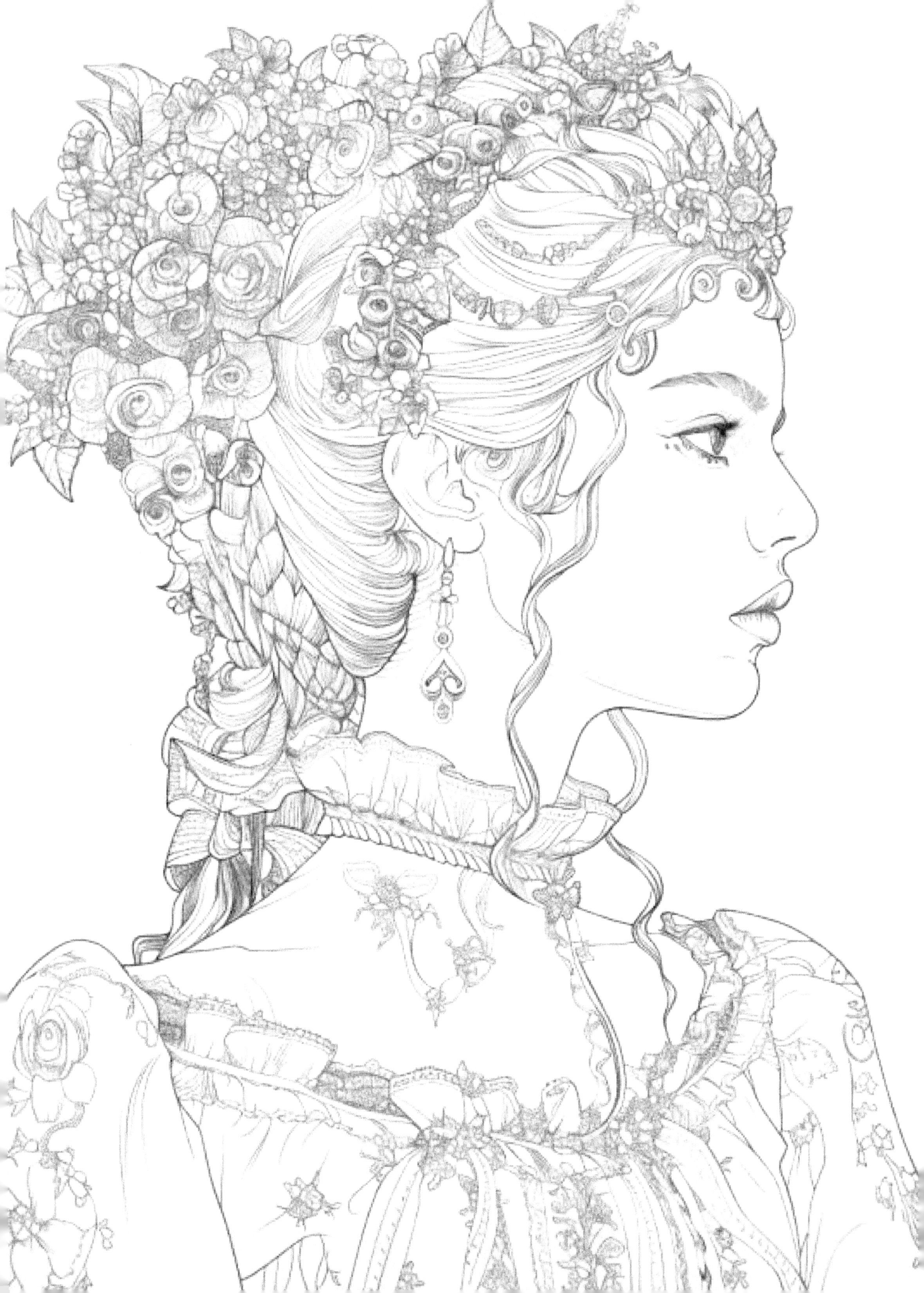

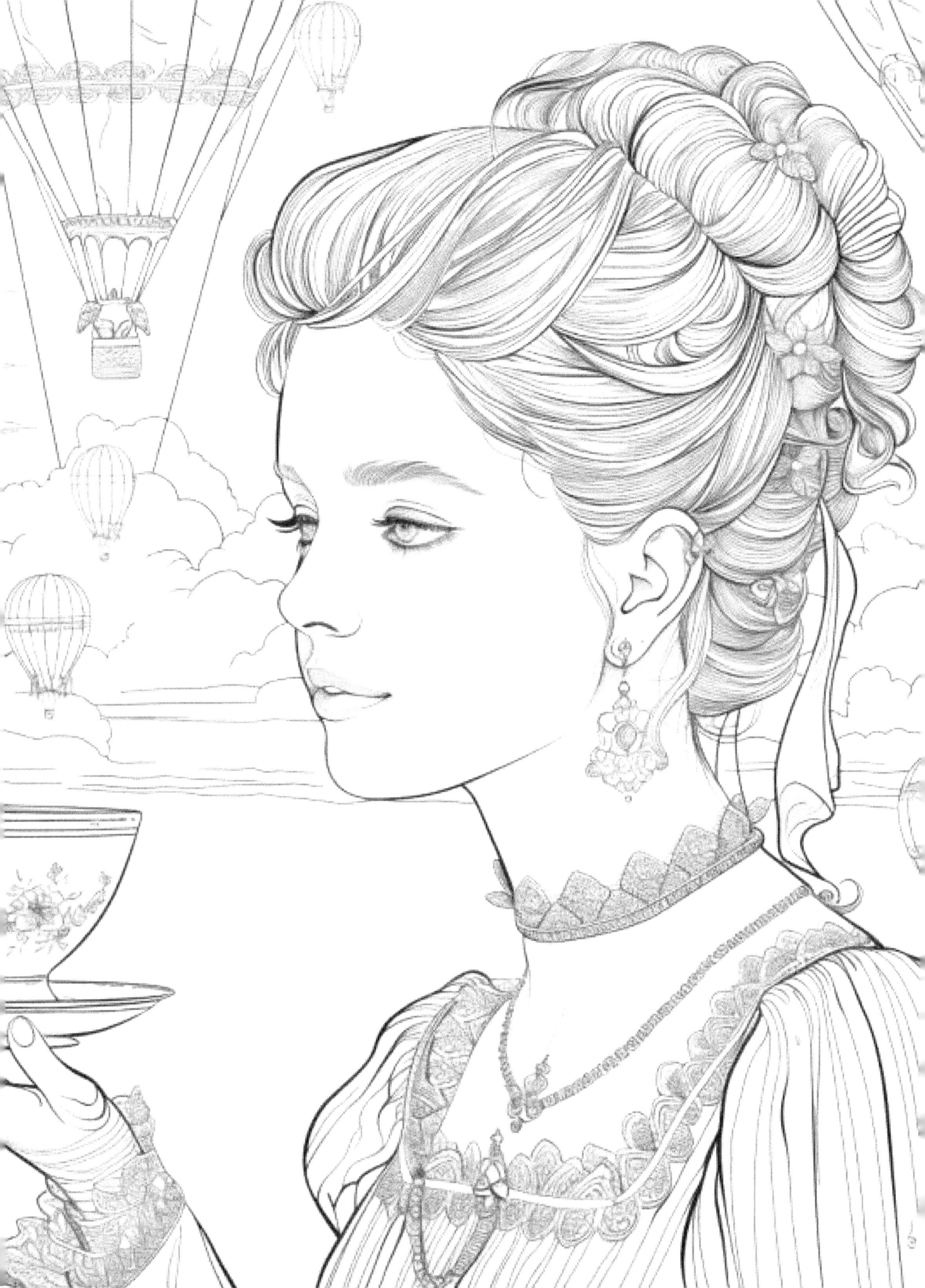

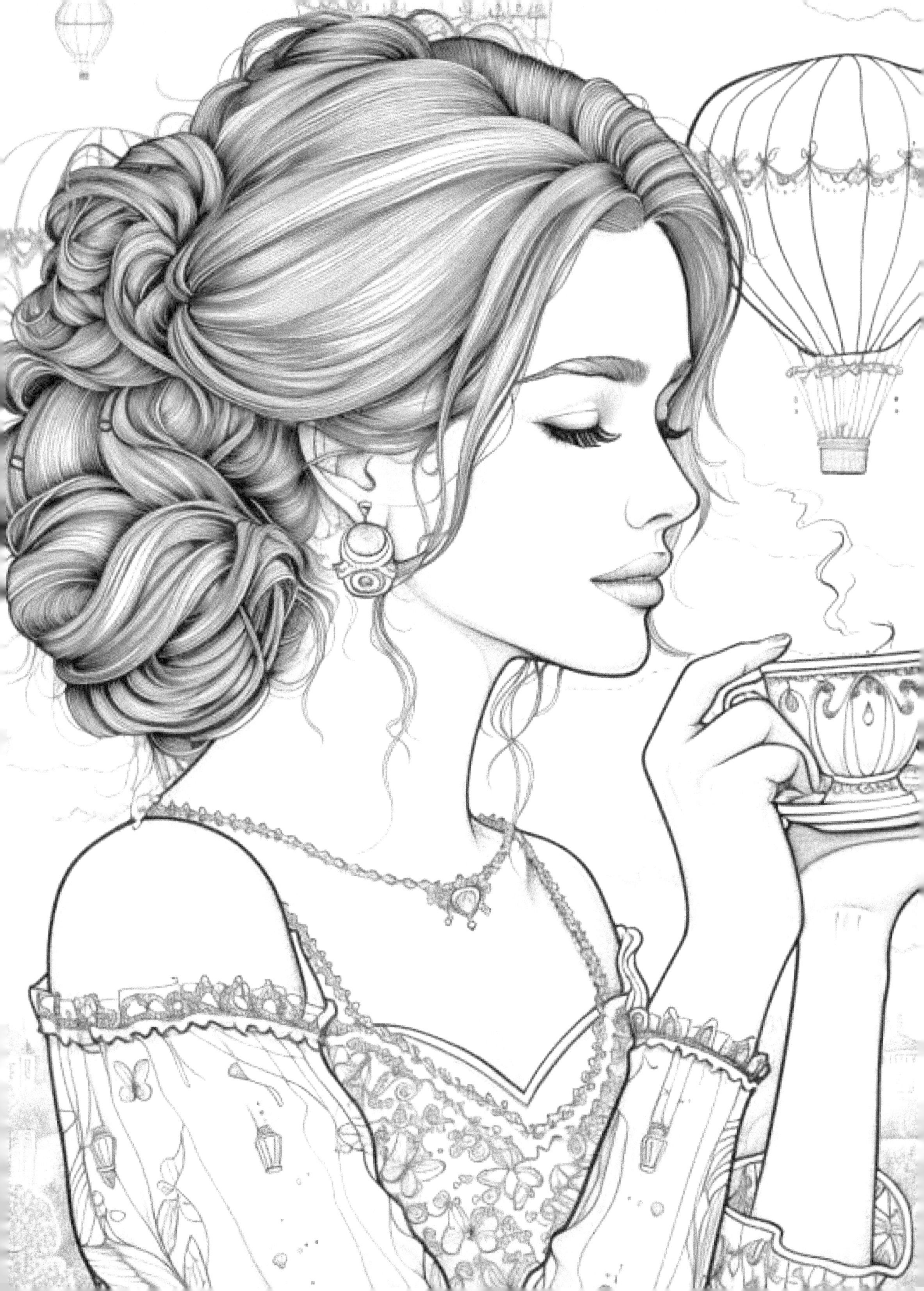

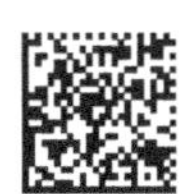